Partnership Tax Planning for Solicitors

Partnership Tax Planning for Solicitors

PANNELL
KERR
FORSTER

CHARTERED ACCOUNTANTS

© Longman Group Ltd 1994

ISBN 0 75200 142 6

Published by
Longman Law, Tax and Finance
Longman Group Ltd
21–27 Lamb's Conduit Street
London WC1N 3NJ

Associated offices
Australia, Hong Kong, Malaysia, Singapore and USA

A CIP catalogue record for this book is available
from the British Library.

Printed in Great Britain by
Progressive Printing UK Ltd

Contents

Introduction

The Finance Act 1994 contains 73 pages of legislation on the new basis of assessment and self-assessment, but this is merely the first instalment as further legislation is to be introduced in the next Finance Bill. Taken together, this legislation will fundamentally change the basis on which self-employed individuals such as solicitors are taxed and the machinery for making returns and tax liabilities. We are in the middle of changes from a system based on Lord Addington's legislation of 1802 to a system of self-assessment modelled on the US system and which has been designed for the next Century.

As would be expected there are transitional provisions and these afford considerable opportunities for tax planning during the run-up to 1997/98 when the new regime will take full effect. And as always, there is also anti-avoidance legislation and problem areas to be negotiated.

We have divided up this book into four parts. Part I provides an introduction to the various changes and identifies planning opportunities and potential problem areas. Part II covers the rules which govern the way that taxable profits and gains are computed. We deal with capital gains tax reliefs which are likely to be relevant to solicitors and we provide a detailed examination of certain transactions which frequently give rise to difficulties. Part III sets out tax considerations which should be borne in mind by solicitors on the key stages of the firm's development. Part IV deals with tax relief for pension policies and planning for retirement.

Where words appear in bold (normally on the first occasion that they appear in a given chapter), this is to indicate that the term is defined in the glossary at the front of the book.

Pannell Kerr Forster
September 1994

Glossary of key terms

Actual basis — this is the same as the 'fiscal year basis', ie a firm is assessed for the profits which it earns in the tax year (see p 4).

Ante-penultimate year — this is the tax year before the penultimate year, ie the year before the tax year which precedes the year of cessation.

Capital allowances — these are allowances given in respect of plant and machinery, industrial buildings and commercial property in Enterprise Zones. In general terms, capital allowances represent a form of relief which corresponds to depreciation (see pp 78–83).

Cash basis — a method of producing accounts which excludes debtors and work in progress and only takes account of cash received (and cash payments made) during the firm's year.

Cessation — there are special rules under the PY basis which apply where a firm ceases to carry on its business. Until 6 April 1997, a cessation may arise because there have been changes in the partners in a firm (ie new partners coming in or partners retiring from the firm). From 6 April 1997 onwards, a cessation will occur only if the firm ceases to carry on its business, and changes in the partners will not in themselves give rise to a cessation (the one exception will be a situation where **all** the partners in a firm cease to be partners).

Closing years' rules — Under the present Schedule D rules, a firm is assessed on the actual basis for the tax year in which it ceases to carry on business. Furthermore, the Inland Revenue have the right to adjust the assessments for the two preceding years so that those years may also be assessed on the actual basis if this produces higher assessments than under the preceding year basis (see pp 16–17).

Continuation election — this is an election which may be made in respect of a change in partners prior to 6 April 1997. Unless the election is made, a change in partners will generally be treated as giving rise to a cessation of the firm for tax purposes whereas the effect of a continuation election is that the change in partners is disregarded and the firm's business is treated as a continuing business (see pp 17–18).

There is a strict time limit for the submission of a continuation election: basically the election needs to be in the hands of the Inspector of Taxes within two years of the change in partners.

A continuation election needs to be signed by all parties, ie all individuals who were partners before the change and all individuals who were partners immediately afterwards.

Conventional basis — accounts may be drawn up on a conventional basis where no allowance is made for work in progress. Accounts drawn up on the conventional basis may differ from cash basis accounts in that the conventional basis will include invoices which have been rendered but not yet paid.

Current year basis — this is the new Schedule D basis of assessment introduced by FA 1994, s 200 whereby an individual will be assessed on his profits for the firm's year which ends in the tax year.

CY basis — this is just another name for current year basis.

Disallowed expenses — these are expenses which are included in commercial accounts, but which do not meet the strict conditions necessary for an expense to be deductible in arriving at Schedule D profits.

Discovery assessments — an Inspector of Taxes may make a discovery where he finds out that he has made a mistake, or his predecessor has made a mistake, or overlooked information in his possession. In such circumstances, an assessment may be made to correct the position (see p 64).

Election to waive VAT exemption — a landlord who lets a property will normally be treated as making exempt supplies for VAT purposes. This means that he cannot recover input VAT. It is possible to make an election to waive the VAT exemption and the landlord can then recover input tax. However, as a consequence of making the election, the landlord will need to charge VAT on the rent. Furthermore, if and when the property is disposed of, he will need to charge VAT at standard rate.

Fiscal year basis — this is just another name for the 'actual basis' ie a person carrying on a trade or profession is assessed according to the profits which he has actually earned during the tax year concerned.

Held-over gain — where an individual or trustee makes a gift of assets which qualifies as business property, an election may be made so that any capital gain for the donor is deferred or 'held-over'. What actually happens is that the gain is not charged on the donor but the donee's capital gains tax base cost is reduced by the amount of the gain. This will normally mean that more tax will be payable when the donee makes a disposal (see TCGA 1992, s 165).

Hold-over relief — this is the relief given to a donor or other transferor of business assets. Where an individual etc. is entitled to hold-over relief, his gain is not charged but is deducted from the asset's market value in determining the transferee's acquisition value for capital gains tax purposes (see TCGA 1992, s 165).

Indexation relief — this is an adjustment made for capital gains tax purposes to allow for inflation (see p 90). The relief is given by means of an adjustment to the disponor's acquisition value for capital gains tax purposes. The adjustment is computed by reference to the increase in the retail price index between the month of acquisition and the month of disposal.

Inland Revenue Audit — under the new self-assessment system, the Inland Revenue will have a right to audit Tax Returns (see p 58). When giving notice that they are commencing an audit, the Revenue will not be required to state any reason.

'New Rules' — this is a colloquial term frequently given to the Schedule D current year basis.

Opening Years' Rules — under the present Schedule D system, there are special rules for computing the assessable profits for the year in which the business commences, and the subsequent tax year. In some cases, the opening years rules also determine the assessment for the third tax year (see pp 5–16).

There are also special rules for the opening years under the CY basis.

Ordinarily resident — this concept normally arises in relation to capital gains tax. An individual may be resident but not ordinarily resident in the UK. Ordinary residence implies a degree of permanence and is approximately the same as *habitual* residence.

Overlap relief — Under the new Schedule D basis of assessment, there are special provisions to cover the way in which profits are assessed for the opening years (see FA 1994, s 205). The general principle is that total amount of profits which are assessed over the life of the business should precisely equal the actual profits earned by the business. Overlap relief covers situations where a particular year's profits are assessed more than once (usually under the opening years rules) and is effectively an adjustment to ensure that this does not result in excessive amounts being assessed overall.

Overlap relief is given by way of a deduction from an individual's profits when he ceases to carry on his business or profession, or when the accounting date of the firm is changed to a date which falls later in the tax year (see pp 5–6 and p 33).

Penultimate year — the tax year immediately preceding the tax year in which a cessation occurs for Schedule D Case II purposes.

Personal Pension Scheme — these are approved pension schemes run by insurance companies, banks, building societies or unit trust groups. An individual who is self-employed or who is in non-pensionable employment may make contributions to a personal pension scheme (see p 175).

Post-cessation receipts — these are amounts received by a person after he has ceased to carry on business and which are assessable as and when he receives them because his business accounts were drawn up on the cash basis (see ICTA 1988, ss 103–104).

Preceding year basis — under the present Schedule D system, which applies for an individual who commenced business prior to 6 April 1994, the normal basis of assessment for a tax year is the preceding year basis, ie the assessment for the tax year 1994/95 will be based on the firm's accounts for a period which ended during the tax year 1993/94 (see pp 14–17).

Premium — where tenant makes a lump sum payment to a landlord, the landlord will normally be assessed under Schedule A on at least part of the lump sum. The tenant may be entitled to relief for a corresponding proportion of the lump sum (see ICTA 1988, s 87).

'Present system' — colloquialism for the preceding year basis of assessment under Schedule D.

PY basis — this is just another name for preceding year basis.

Qualifying loan interest — an individual who is a partner in a professional firm is entitled to relief for interest paid on qualifying loans, ie loans used to acquire an interest in the firm or loans which have been taken to enable the individual to make a loan to his firm for use in the ordinary course of the firm's business (see p 142).

Relevant earnings — Schedule D profits and earnings from a non-pensionable employment. An individual may make contributions into a personal pension scheme based on a percentage of his relevant earnings for a tax year (see pp 177–178).

Rebasing — this is a technical term for capital gains tax purposes whereby an individual who held an asset at 31 March 1982 may have his capital gain computed as if his cost were the market value of the asset at 31 March 1982 (see p 88).

Repairing a Return — where the Inland Revenue Officer spots an obvious mistake, such as an arithmetical error, he may correct a self-assessment by making a repair (see p 58).

Repayment supplement — this is (tax free) interest paid on a repayment of overpaid tax.

Representative partner — under the new self-assessment regime, a representative partner will need to file a return on behalf of the firm, and all correspondence will be routed by the Revenue through that particular partner (see p 62).

Resident — an individual will generally be regarded as resident in the UK if he is physically present in this country for more than 182 days in a tax year or if he is present in this country for an average of more than 91 days per annum over a four year period.

Retirement annuity policy — these are similar to personal pension schemes. In effect, they are approved contracts under which a person who was self-employed or in non-pensionable employment could provide for their retirement prior to the introduction of personal pension schemes in July 1988. Many retirement annuity policies make provision for premiums to be paid in subsequent years and, whilst no new retirement annuity policies are now issued, contributions under existing policies will thus continue to attract relief for some years to come (see p 180).

Retirement relief — this is a special relief for capital gains tax purposes which applies where an individual disposes of his business or an interest in a business (eg an interest in a firm) (see p 187).

Roll-over relief — this is a capital gains tax relief which applies where an individual disposes of a business or an asset used in a business and spends the proceeds on acquiring replacement assets during a qualifying period (normally up to one year before and up to three years after the date of disposal of the original asset) (see p 91).

Salaried partner — a salaried partner is an individual who is subject to the supervision and direction of equity partners and who is therefore no more than a very senior employee. Salaried partners are assessable under Schedule E rather than under Schedule D (see p 152).

Schedule D Case II — individuals who carry on a profession are assessed under Schedule D Case II.

Schedule D Case III — this is the charging section under which the Inland Revenue assess interest and other annual payments received by individuals.

Surcharge — this will be a fixed penalty which will be added to tax which is paid late under the self-assessment regime (see p 61).

Terminal loss relief — losses realised by an individual during the final 12 months of his business may be carried back and set against profits for the previous 36 months (see p 186).

Timing differences — some amounts which are charged in accounts may not be allowable at that point in time. However, if tax relief will be available in due course, there is said to be a timing difference (see p 72).

Transitional basis — where a firm has been assessed on the PY basis for 1995/96, the firm will normally be assessed under the transitional basis for 1996/97. In practice, this normally means that the assessment for 1996/97 will be based on 12 month's share of the profits for a period commencing immediately after the end of the basis period for 1995/96 and ending on the date to which accounts are drawn up during the tax year 1996/97 (see p 22 and FA 1994, Sched 20, paras 1–6).

Transitional relief — where an individual was previously assessed under the preceding year basis, transitional relief may be due in respect of the amount assessed for 1997/98 covering the proportion of that assessment which relates to the period prior to 6 April 1997. The relief is given in the same way as overlap relief (see p 24 and FA 1994, Sched 20, para 2). The Inland Revenue refer to the basis period for 1997/98 as the **transitional relief period**.

Transitional year basis period — The period from the day after the end of the 1995/96 basis period up to the date to which accounts are made up during the tax year 1996/97 (see p 22). The Inland Revenue sometimes refer to this as the **transitional basis period**.

Triggers — these are various events or changes which may enable the Inland Revenue to invoke anti-avoidance rules and assess additional amounts for either 1995/96 or 1996/97.

Table of Statutes

Part I

Planning for the new Schedule D regime

The most important change for solicitors is the new rules for determining taxable profits (the current year basis). It should also be noted that the self-assessment regime will come into force in 1996/97 (although some of the record-keeping requirements are already in operation). We deal with self-assessment in Chapter 5.

1   The 'New rules' — and when they apply

2   How the changes will affect you if you were in practice at 5 April 1994

3   Changes in accounting date

4   Tax planning and anti-avoidance provisions

5   Self-assessment from 1996/97 — how this will affect solicitors

Chapter 1

The 'New Rules' — and when they apply

In this chapter we address the following matters:

> - How the new rules will affect solicitors who set up in practice on or after 6 April 1994;
> - How the new rules could apply to a partner;
> - Treatment of partnership interest and other investment income;
> - The position on a change in accounting date or retirement;
> - Capital allowances;
> - Expenses incurred by partners on an individual basis.

How the new rules will affect sole practitioners who commence on or after 6 April 1994

Whereas an individual in a practice which commenced before 6 April 1994 will normally be assessed on the 'preceding year' or **PY basis** for 1995/96, on a **transitional basis** for 1996/97 and will come on to the current year basis in 1997/98, a solicitor who commences to practice on or after 6 April 1994 will come under the new current year basis immediately (FA 1994, s 200).

Current year basis of assessment

In broad terms, the **current year basis of assessment** (also called the 'CY basis') will normally mean that a solicitor is assessed on the profits for his firm's year which ends in the tax year concerned (there are special rules for the opening years). Thus, if a solicitor makes up accounts to 31 August, the CY basis of assessment will normally mean that his tax assessment for 1996/97 will be determined by his profits for the year ending 31 August 1996.

However, the CY basis needs special rules to cope with a business during the first two tax years since there may not be an accounting year which ends in either of those tax years or the accounting period which ends in the second tax year may be shorter or longer than 12 months.

In broad terms, assessments will generally be determined as follows:

- First tax year — actual or fiscal year basis;
- Second tax year — profits of the first 12 months;
- Third tax year — current year basis.

EXAMPLE

Peter starts in business on 6 October 1994. His accounts for the year to 5 October 1995 show profits of £48,000. Profits for the year ending 5 October 1996 are £72,000.

Peter will be assessed as follows:

	£
1994/95 — 'actual' basis ($^6/_{12}$ × £48,000)	24,000
1995/96 — First 12 months profits	48,000
1996/97 — Current year basis	72,000

The precise way in which the opening year rules work is slightly more complicated where the practice does not prepare accounts for a period of 12 months ending in the second tax year. The flow chart below and the worked examples at the end of this chapter (Appendix 1) show how the assessments will be made if you fall within this category.

Overlap relief

Because of the way that a new business is assessed during the first two tax years, some profits may be taxed more than once. To

BASIS OF ASSESSMENT UNDER OPENING YEARS RULES

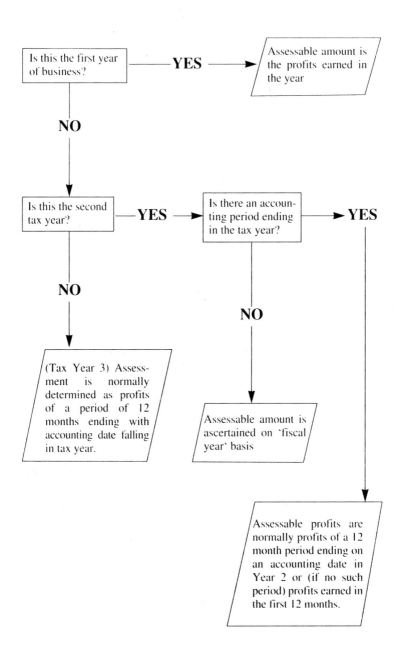

compensate for this, and to ensure that over the life of the business tax is paid only on the actual amount of profits, overlap relief is given when the business is discontinued or, in the case of partners, when they leave the firm (FA 1994, s 205). In some circumstances, overlap relief may also be available if the firm's accounting date is changed (see Chapter 3).

EXAMPLE

In the above example, $^6/_{12}$ of the first 12 months' profits are assessed twice. Accordingly, a figure of £24,000 is carried forward and is deducted from Peter's profits for the final year of trading.

Thus, if Peter retires on 5 October 1998, and his final year's profits are £60,000, the assessment for 1998/99 will be as follows:

	£
Current year basis	60,000
Less overlap relief	24,000
Taxable profits	36,000

If the overlap relief exceeds the taxable profits for the final year, the balance may be treated as an allowable loss and either set against the individual's other income for that year or the preceding year, or carried back against Schedule D Case II profits of the last three years (**terminal loss relief**).

How the new rules could apply to a partner

Where a firm of solicitors has been in existence for a number of years, the partners will normally be assessed on the preceding year basis. The fact that a new partner joins, or an existing partner retires, does not necessarily mean that the old partnership is deemed to have come to an end for tax purposes. However, this will be the situation unless all the partners join in a **continuation election** under ICTA 1988, s 113(2). If no election is made, or if a provisional election is submitted but then withdrawn during the two year period allowed by the legislation, the old partnership is deemed to have ceased and a new firm come into being.

In a situation like this, and where the change in partners occurs after 5 April 1994, the new partnership is treated as if it were a wholly new business. This means:

- Partners will be assessed individually;
- The partners' shares of profits will be assessed under the new CY basis.

Partners assessed individually

Where the CY basis applies to a partnership, assessments will always be made on the individual partners rather than on the firm itself. Each partner is responsible for settling his own tax liabilities and is not jointly and severally liable for the total amount of tax payable by the partners. There may be a small exception to this where there are non-resident partners in the firm.

Application of the CY basis to partners

Basically, each partner is treated independently and the rules outlined on p 4 are applied to him.

EXAMPLE

Kenneth and Jon start a new practice on 6 October 1994. They share profits equally. On 6 January 1996, Valerie joins them and takes a ⅓ entitlement to profits.

Accounts to 5 October 1995 show a profit of £132,000. The accounts for the years to 5 October 1996 and 5 October 1997 show a profit of £240,000 and £300,000 respectively.

The position is as follows:

1994/95

Kenneth and Jon are each assessed on the actual basis ie the firm's profits of £66,000 for 1994/95 ($^6/_{12}$ × £132,000 profits for the year ended 5 October 1995) are divided equally between them. Kenneth and Jon are therefore each assessed on £33,000.

1995/96

Kenneth and Jon are assessed on their share of the firm's profits for the first 12 months, ie profits of £132,000 are divided equally and each is assessed on £66,000.

Valerie is assessed on the actual basis, because 1995/96 is her first tax year as a partner in this firm, so she is assessed on £20,000 ($\frac{3}{9}$ × her $\frac{1}{3}$ share of the profits for the year ended 5 October 1996).

1996/97

Kenneth and Jon are assessed on the CY basis on their share of the firm's profits for the year ended 5 October 1996, ie £90,000 each ($\frac{1}{2}$ × profits for 3 months + $\frac{1}{3}$ × profits for 9 months).

Valerie is assessed on the profits for her first 12 months, ie £85,000 ($\frac{9}{12}$ × £80,000 plus $\frac{3}{12}$ × £100,000).

1997/98

All three partners are assessed on the CY basis, ie their $\frac{1}{3}$ share of the firm's profits for the year ended 5 October 1997 of £300,000.

Similarly, the provisions on overlap relief are applied separately in relation to each partner. Thus, in the above example, if Kenneth retired on 5 October 1997, he will be entitled to overlap relief in arriving at his taxable profits for 1997/98. The other on-going partners would get their overlap relief only when they retire or the firm ceases business or changes its accounting date — see below. Their overlap relief is as follows:

	£	
Kenneth	33,000	
Jon	33,000	
Valerie	25,000	($\frac{3}{12}$ × £100,000).

Treatment of partnership interest and other investment income

A partner may be entitled to a share of interest earned by the firm on surplus cash — or indeed any other investment income. Each partner is assessed on his share of such income, but it is assessed on the CY basis (see FA 1994, s 215). Thus, if a firm makes up accounts to 31 May, the partners will be assessed for 1996/97 on their share of investment income in the firm's accounts for the year ended 31 May 1996. This can give rise to some anomalies since the relevant income may actually have been received during the tax year 1995/96.

Change in accounting date/retirement

The CY basis requires special adjustments to be made where there is a change in the firm's accounting date (see FA 1994, s 202). There are also special rules for arriving at taxable income under the CY basis for a tax year in which an individual ceases business.

Change in accounting date

Where a firm changes its accounting date to a date which falls earlier in the tax year, an adjustment is required in order to ensure that 12 months' profits are taxed as income of the year in which the change takes place.

EXAMPLE

Marilyn is in practice. She draws up accounts to 30 June. However, in 1997, she changes to a 30 April accounting date. This means that her accounts which fall in 1997/98 are for a period of only 10 months.

The CY basis requires profits to be ascertained for a 12 month period which ends with the new accounting date. Suppose that the relevant figures were:

Year ended 30 June 1996 — profits of £120,000

Period of 10 months ended 30 April 1997 — profits of £140,000

Marilyn would be assessed for 1997/98 on £160,000 ie $\frac{2}{12}$ × profits for the year ended 30 June 1996 plus profits for the 10 months ended 30 April 1997.

Once again, some profits will have been taxed more than once and therefore Marilyn would be entitled to increased overlap relief in due course on $\frac{2}{12}$ of the profits for the year ended 30 June 1996. This overlap relief is enjoyed as and when the firm's accounting date is changed to a date which falls later in the tax year or Marilyn retires from practice.

A different approach is required in cases where a firm extends its accounts to a date which falls later in the tax year. Normally, the assessable profits will be the profits for the entire period which ends in the tax year.

EXAMPLE

Mike and Gillian make up accounts to 31 December. They share profits equally. In 1998, they extend their accounting period so that the firm has a 15 month accounting period from 1 January 1997 to 31 March 1998.

The whole of the profits for this period are assessed for 1997/98, but Mike and Gillian can use some or all of their overlap relief. Suppose that Mike and Gillian each have a potential entitlement to four months overlap relief of £20,000. Also assume that the profits for the 15 months ended 31 March 1998 are £300,000.

Mike and Gillian would each have Schedule D Case II income for 1997/98 of £135,000, ie

	£
Half-share of profits	150,000
Less $\frac{3 \text{ months}}{4 \text{ months}}$ × overlap relief brought forward	15,000
	135,000

Retirement

A different rule applies where a solicitor ceases to carry on a practice or where he ceases to be a partner in a professional firm. The individual will be taxed under the CY basis on his profits for a notional period which starts immediately after the basis period for the previous tax year and ends on the date that he ceases (see FA 1994, s 204).

EXAMPLE

Adrian and Louise are in partnership, sharing profits equally. They make up accounts to 30 April. Their profits for the year ended 30 April 1998 are £80,000.

Louise retires from the firm on 30 November 1998. The firm's profits for the year ended 30 April 1999 are £100,000.

Louise's assessable income for 1998/99 is her share of profits for the period 1 May 1997–30 November 1998, ie one half of £80,000 plus one half of $\frac{6}{12}$ × £100,000.

Thus, for 1997/98, Adrian is taxed on £40,000 and Louise is taxed on £65,000 (less any overlap relief brought forward from previous years).

Capital allowances

Under the new rules (see FA 1994, ss 211–212), the basis period for capital allowances will always be the same as for determining profits — even in the opening years.

Furthermore, capital allowances will be treated as if they were an expense, and deducted in arriving at the Schedule D Case II profits for a period rather than a deduction from profits assessable for a tax year as has been the case hitherto.

Opening years

The operation of the new rules is best explained by an example.

EXAMPLE

Assume that Alan started his practice on 1 July 1994 and accounts are drawn up to 30 June 1995. If the profits before capital allowances amount to £48,000, and capital allowances amount to £6,000 the net profits are taken as £42,000. The position will then be as follows:

	£
1994/95 — actual basis ie $\frac{9}{12}$ × £42,000 =	31,500
1995/96 — first 12 months	42,000

It should be noted that the above treatment would still apply even if the allowances of £6,000 relate wholly to expenditure incurred in the period 6 April–30 June 1995.

Expenses incurred by partners on an individual basis

It sometimes happens that solicitors submit expense claims on an individual basis, and the Inspector will then deduct the relevant amounts from the solicitor's share of the partnership profits based on accounts which do not take in such expenses. However, the Revenue have never been comfortable with this approach and it will not be possible to do this after 1995/96 — see Chapter 5 on the self-assessment which will apply from 1996/97 onwards.

Appendix 1 — worked examples of CY basis opening years' rules

Example 1 — first set of accounts cover a period of less than 12 months

Peter and Norma start in practice on 1 January 1995. The first set of accounts are made up to 30 April 1995, then to 30 April 1996.

Peter and Norma will be assessed on profits computed as follows:

1994/95 — $\frac{3}{4}$ × profits of period 1 January–30 April 1995.

1995/96 — fiscal year basis, ie
$\frac{1}{4}$ × profits of period 1 January–30 April 1995

Plus $\frac{11}{12}$ × profits for year ended 30 April 1996.

Example 2 — No accounts ending in second tax year

Sara and Beverley start in practice on 1 March 1995 and the first set of accounts are made up to 30 April 1996.

Their assessable profits are:

1994/95 — $\frac{1}{14}$ × profits for 14 months ended 30 April 1996.

1995/96 — $\frac{12}{14}$ × profits for 14 months ended 30 April 1996.

1996/97 — $\frac{12}{14}$ × profits for 14 months ended 30 April 1996.

Chapter 2

How the changes will affect you if you were in practice at 5 April 1994

In this chapter, we look at solicitors who started in practice before the start of the tax year 1994/95, whether as sole practitioners or partners in a firm. We address the following questions which commonly arise in discussions with solicitors:

- How are your profits assessed under the present system?
- How will this change in 1997/98?
- How will 1996/97 profits be assessed?
- What will happen if a new partner is admitted before 6 April 1997?
- What will be the tax implications of a partner leaving the firm before 6 April 1999?
- How does your firm provide for tax in its accounts?

How are your profits assessed under the present system?

The way in which you are assessed at present will depend upon when you commenced practice, (if you are a sole practitioner) or when you last had a 'cessation' for tax purposes (if you are a partner).

If you are a sole practitioner

You will be assessed for 1994/95 on the **preceding year basis** (or 'PY' basis) unless you started to practice after 5 April 1993. If 1994/95 is assessed on the PY basis, the assessment for 1995/96 will normally be on the PY basis as well.

If you are assessed on the PY basis, you will be charged tax for 1994/95 on your profits for your accounts year which ended in the tax year 1993/94. Thus, if you have a 30 September year end, the PY basis will mean that you will be assessed for the tax year 1994/95 on your profits for the year ended 30 September 1993. Similarly, you will be assessed for 1995/96 on your profits for the year ended 30 September 1994.

If you started to practice after 5 April 1993, you will normally be subject to the **'opening years'** rules. Basically, the present tax system provides that a solicitor should be assessed on the **'actual basis'** for the first tax year in which he practices and he is normally assessed for the second tax year on his profits for the first 12 months.

EXAMPLE

Daniel commenced on 5 July 1993. His profits for the year ended 5 July 1994 were £36,000 and his profits for the following year were £48,000.

His 1993/94 assessment will be on the actual profits earned during the tax year, ie 9/12ths × £36,000 = £27,000.

The 1994/95 assessment will be on £36,000. The 1995/96 assessment will normally be on the PY basis, ie £36,000.

There is an exception to the above for practitioners who started on 6 April. Thus, if Daniel had started his practice on 6 April 1993, his assessment would be:

1993/94 — actual profits earned in the tax year
1994/95 — PY basis

There is another potential complication; a sole practitioner may choose to have the assessments for his second and third tax years determined by the actual profits earned in those years.

EXAMPLE

Laurence commenced business on 1 June 1993 and makes up accounts to 31 May. His profits are as follows:

	£
Year ended 31 May 1994 (first year)	£30,000
Year ended 31 May 1995	£18,000
Year ended 31 May 1996	£36,000

Under the normal rules, Laurence will be assessed as follows:

	£
1993/94 — 'actual', ie 10/12ths × £30,000 =	25,000
1994/95 — first 12 months' profits	30,000
1995/96 — PY basis	30,000

If Laurence so elects, the assessments for the second and third tax years will be as follows:

	£
1994/95 — 2/12 × £30,000	5,000
10/12 × £18,000	15,000
	20,000
1995/96 — 2/12 £18,000	3,000
10/12 × £36,000	30,000
	33,000

It should be noted that a sole practitioner must either elect for both the second and third tax years to be assessed on the actual basis, or he can allow the normal rules to take effect, but he cannot 'pick and choose'. Thus, Laurence cannot elect for 1994/95 to be assessed on the actual basis and 1995/96 on the PY basis.

Closing years rules

When a cessation occurs, the firm's profits for the tax year in which the cessation takes place are assessed on the actual basis. Furthermore, the Inland Revenue has the option of adjusting the assessments for the two preceding years (the 'penultimate' tax year and the 'antepenultimate' year). Once again, the Revenue must either adjust both years or neither, they cannot pick and choose by simply amending one year in isolation.

EXAMPLE

Alex ceases to practice on 31 March 1995.

His profits have been:

	£
Year ended 31 March 1992	30,000
Year ended 31 March 1993	28,000
Year ended 31 March 1994	50,000
Year ended 31 March 1995	40,000

The existing assessments for the antepenultimate and penultimate years will be:

	£
1992/93	30,000
1993/94	28,000

The Revenue will adjust these assessments as follows:

	£	
1992/93	28,000	Actual basis
1993/94	50,000	Actual basis

The profits assessable for 1994/95 will be £40,000, ie the final tax year is always assessed on the actual basis.

If you are a partner

Under the present system, there is a notional **cessation** every time a partner joins or leaves a firm, with the 'old firm' being deemed to have ceased and a new firm deemed to start a practice. However, it is possible to override this rule by the partners making a **'continuation election'**. This election has to be signed by all parties concerned (ie all the individuals previously in partnership and any incoming partners) and submitted to the Inspector of Taxes within two years of the change in partners. In effect, the submission of the continuation election means that the change in partners does not affect the computation of profits assessed on the firm.

In cases where continuation elections are made on all partnership changes, a firm will generally be assessed on the PY basis for 1994/95 and 1995/96. The assessments are made as if the firm were an on-going group of persons and the assessable profits are divided amongst the individual partners in accordance with the way in which they share profits for the tax year concerned.

EXAMPLE

Marie and Anthea have been in partnership for a number of years and are assessed on the PY basis. At the start of the firm's year ended 31 March 1995, Louise joins them as a partner. A continuation election is made. Partners share profits equally throughout.

The firm's profits are:

	£
Year ended 31 March 1993	73,000
Year ended 31 March 1994	72,000
Year ended 31 March 1995	96,000
Year ended 31 March 1996	120,000

Because the continuation election has been made, the firm is assessed as follows:

1993/94 — PY basis £73,000 (Louise is treated as having 5 days' worth of profits — ie $\frac{5}{365} \times \frac{1}{3} \times$ £73,000)

1994/95 — PY basis £72,000 (the profits are treated as arising equally between the partners so Louise is regarded as having taxable income of £24,000)

1995/96   PY basis £96,000

If no continuation election were made, (or if a provisional continuation election were withdrawn before the two year time limit expires) the enlarged firm of Marie, Anthea and Louise will be assessed as follows:

		£
1993/94 — 'actual basis' ie	$\frac{5}{365} \times$ £96,000	1,315
1994/95 — first 12 months		96,000
1995/96 — PY basis		96,000

An assessment would also be made for 1993/94 on the old partnership.

Anti-avoidance provisions

Many professional firms took full advantage of the above rules by having cessations and notional commencements of a new firm so as to minimise their tax liabilities. Accordingly, the legislation was amended in 1986 and now provides that if there is a notional cessation (because of a new partner joining a practice or a partner retiring from the firm) and a continuation election could have been made, but was not made, the profits of the new firm are assessed on the actual basis for the first four tax years.

EXAMPLE

Stuart and John have been in partnership for a number of years. On 6 October 1992, a new partner (Steven) joined them. No continuation election was made.

The firm's results are:

	£
Year ended 5 October 1992	100,000
Year ended 5 October 1993	120,000
Year ended 5 October 1994	270,000
Year ended 5 October 1995	300,000

The normal rules would mean that the firm would be assessed as follows:

	£
1992/93 — actual basis $\frac{6}{12}$ × £120,000	60,000
1993/94 — First 12 months	120,000
1994/95 — PY basis	120,000
1995/96 — PY basis	270,000

Because of the anti-avoidance rules, the new firm is assessed on an actual basis for these years, ie

	£
1992/93 — As above	60,000
1993/94 — $^6/_{12}$ × £120,000	60,000
$^6/_{12}$ × £270,000	135,000
	195,000
1994/95 — $^6/_{12}$ × £270,000	135,000
$^6/_{12}$ × £300,000	150,000
	285,000
1995/96 — $^6/_{12}$ × 300,000	150,000
$^6/_{12}$ × 330,000	165,000
	315,000

How the basis of assessment will change in 1997/98

Sole practitioners and partners in professional firms (and, indeed, all unincorporated businesses) will be taxed under Schedule D on the current year basis (CY) for 1997/98 and future years (see FA 1994, Sched 20). This basically means that assessments will be made on the profits for the firm's year which ends in the tax year. Thus, a sole practitioner who makes up accounts to 30 April 1997 will be assessed for 1997/98 as if those profits were earned wholly in that tax year.

Similarly, partners in a professional firm with a year end of 30 November will be assessed on their share of the firm's profits for the year ended 30 November 1997.

There will be one other change for partners in that as from 1997/98 onwards, assessments will be made on the individual partners rather than on the firm. Moreover, partners will no longer be jointly and severally liable for the firm's tax but will be responsible only for paying tax on their share of the firm's profits.

How 1996/97 will be assessed

The way in which the assessable profits for 1996/97 will be arrived at depends upon whether your practice/firm is assessed for 1995/96 on the PY basis.

If your firm is presently on the PY basis, so that 1995/96 will be assessed by reference to your firm's profits for a period ending in the tax year 1994/95, the 1996/97 assessment will be based on the average of profits for a period (the '**transitional year basis period**'). This period starts on the day following the end of the basis period for 1995/96 and ends on the day to which accounts are made up during 1996/97. Thus, if you make up accounts to 30 June, the basis period for 1995/96 will normally be the year ended 30 June 1994 and the transitional basis period will be the two year period starting on 1 July 1994 and ending on 30 June 1996.

Where the transitional year basis period is a period of 24 months, the 1996/97 assessment will be arrived at by taking 12/24ths of the profits for that two year period.

In some cases, the 1996/97 assessment may be based on 12 months proportion of a period which exceeds two years. Thus, if you have a 30 April year end at present, but your firm switches to 31 March during 1997, the 1996/97 assessment will be based on 12/35ths × the profits for the 35 month period 1 May 1994–31 March 1997.

Position if 1995/96 is assessed on the actual basis

It could well happen that a firm is assessed on the actual basis for 1995/96, perhaps because there was a cessation during the period 6 April 1992–5 April 1994 because of a change in partners with no continuation election being made.

If 1995/96 is assessed on the actual basis, the same will apply for 1996/97.

Implications of admitting a new partner before 6 April 1997

The present rules under which a change in partners may be treated as giving rise to a cessation are still in force and this will continue to be the case up to 5 April 1997. This means, in effect, that if your firm admits a partner before the start of the tax year 1997/98, and no continuation election is made, the firm is deemed to have ceased to practice. This will mean that the Revenue will amend the firm's assessment for the year in which the cessation is deemed to take place and the Revenue may also have the right to adjust the assessments for the two preceding years.

The rules set out in Chapter 1 will then apply to the on-going partners as if they had commenced a completely new practice from the date of the change of partners. Thus, if there is a change in partners between now and 1997/98, the on-going partners could have two assessments for the year of the change, one reflecting

actual profits up to the date of the deemed cessation and another
assessment under the new rules.

Implications of a partner retiring before 6 April 1999

There will be certain key differences as between a partner retiring
before 6 April 1997 and after that date but before 6 April 1999.

Partner retiring before 6 April 1997

The retirement of a partner before 1997/98 may be treated as a
change in partners which gives rise to a cessation for tax purposes.
The only way to avoid this is for all the parties to join in a
continuation election.

Partner retiring between 6 April 1997 and 5 April 1999

A change in partners after 5 April 1997 will not be treated as
a cessation unless all the partners retire and the business actually
comes to an end. If such a cessation occurs, the Revenue may
be able to adjust the assessments for 1995/96 and 1996/97 (if the
cessation occurs in 1997/98) or for 1996/97 only (if the cessation
occurs in 1997/98).

It should normally be possible to prevent a cessation where the
tax consequences would be unwelcome provided the firm's business
is still viable.

EXAMPLE

If Louise and Catherine are in practice together, and they
plan to hand over to Lesley in 1997/98 and then retire,
they could deal with this in one of two ways.

They could sell Lesley the practice so that their
partnership came to an end on the day of the sale —
this could be the occasion of a cessation.

Alternatively, they could admit Lesley as a partner during
1997/98 and then retire (possibly a few weeks later). This
would not give rise to a cessation and Louise and
Catherine would be safe from any adjustments to their
1995/96 and 1996/97 assessments **provided** Lesley

continues to carry on the practice and does not have a
cessation before 6 April 1999.

Where a partner retires, his income for the year of retirement will
be ascertained as follows. The whole amount of profits earned up
to the date of retirement since the end of the basis period for the
previous tax year are assessable for the year of retirement. Thus,
if Alan has been a partner in a firm with a 30 September year
end, and he retires on 31 December 1998, his 1998/99 profits will
be the amount earned during the period 1 October 1997–31
December 1998, ie profits of a period of 15 months. However,
the effect of this may be mitigated by transitional relief (see below).

Transitional relief

A proportion of the profits for the firm's year which ends in 1997/98
will be allowed as a deduction by way of transitional relief against
an individual's assessable profits for the year in which he retires
(FA 1994, Sched 20, para 2).

EXAMPLE

Jon and Steve share profits equally. They make up
accounts to 5 May. Their profits for the year ended 5
May 1997 amount to £120,000.

For 1997/98 each would be assessed on £60,000.

When either partner retires, transitional relief of £55,000
will be available, ie $^{11}/_{12}$ths × £60,000 (the profits for the
period 6 May 1996–5 May 1997).

Transitional relief also applies where a partnership has interest or
other investment income which, after 5 April 1997, will be taxed
on the CY basis (see p 3)
    If transitional relief exceeds the profits assessable for the year
of retirement, the balance will be available to be relieved in the
same way as loss relief, ie by off-set against the individual's other
income for the year, or his other income for the preceding year,
or by way of terminal loss relief by carry-back against earlier years'
profits from that business.
    Transitional relief may be allowed earlier than this if the
accounting date of the business is changed to a date later in the

tax year. Where there is a change in accounting date after 5 April 1997, transitional relief may be used as if it were overlap relief (see example on p 33).

How does your firm provide for tax in its accounts?

If you are a sole practitioner, you can provide for tax in any way you please — this is basically a matter between you and your accountant.

If you are a partner, the possibilities are once again legion. Because a partnership does not have to draw up accounts which conform with the Companies Acts or other legislation, it is really open to the partners as to how they want to provide for tax liabilities. Some partnership deeds even provide that partners who retire should receive their share of the profits for their final year with no deduction for tax whatsoever.

It is not uncommon, particularly where a family firm is concerned, for the annual accounts to simply make a provision for the tax payable up to the point in the tax year in which the accounts end. On this approach (the 'minimum liability basis') if your year end is 31 May, the firm's accounts to 31 May 1994 will contain a provision for the tax payable in January 1994 in respect of the tax year 1993/94. However, this is the bare minimum and many firms would provide for the second instalment of the 1993/94 tax due for payment on 1 July 1994. A more common policy is to provide for tax on the 'all profits earned basis'. Thus, in the case of a firm with accounts made up to 31 July 1994, the tax provision would include a provision for the tax due on the firm's Schedule D Case II assessment for 1995/96 (tax payable 1 January and 1 July 1996).

The weakness with this approach is that further tax may be payable if partners retire, because of the cessation provisions. Furthermore, even though the firm may continue, it would not be appropriate for a partner to be paid out all his profits without making any deduction for additional tax which may be payable if the firm subsequently has a cessation. Accordingly most large firms have adopted the 'discontinuance basis'.

This basis requires a provision to be made for the **maximum** tax which could become payable if the firm had a cessation for tax purposes. Each year, as it becomes clear that a cessation has not occurred which could affect the assessment for an earlier year, part of the provision is written back as it is surplus to requirements.

A firm which provides for tax in this way will need to bear in mind the possible implications for 1995/96 of a complete cessation in 1997/98. If a cessation occurs in 1997/98, the Revenue may be able to adjust the 1995/96 assessment so that the profits assessed are the actual profits earned in that year. If a cessation occurs in 1998/99, the Revenue may be able to assess additional profits for 1996/97 (1995/96 will then be outside the scope of the **closing years rules**).

From 1997/98 onwards, partners will be assessed individually and will not be jointly liable for the firm's tax. This will clearly make things much easier in that the choice of how conservatively to provide for tax will be a personal matter for each partner. As it becomes plain that a cessation will not occur before 6 April 1999, surplus tax provisions for years up to 1996/97 should be released to the partners.

BUSINESS COMMENCED PRE 6 APRIL 1994
DETERMINING ASSESSABLE PROFITS FOR SCHEDULE D
CASES I AND II YEARS 1994/95 — 1996/97

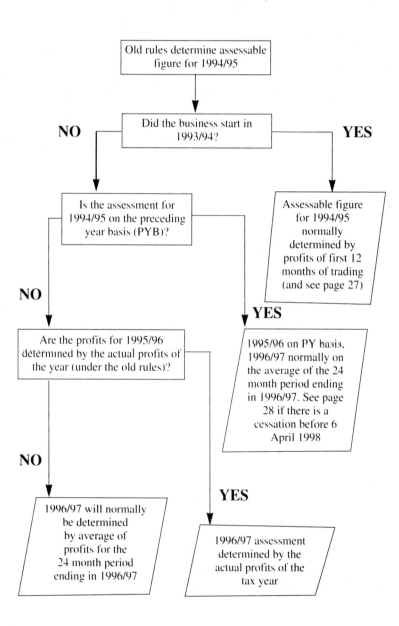

BUSINESS COMMENCED IN 1993/94 DETERMINING ASSESSABLE PROFITS FOR SCHEDULE D CASES I AND II YEARS 1994/95 — 1996/97

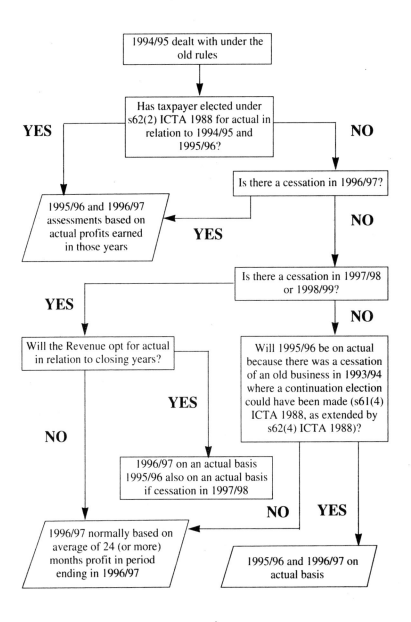

CESSATION BEFORE 6 APRIL 1998

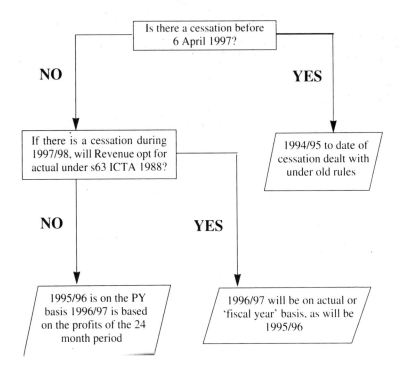

Chapter 3

Changes in accounting date

In this chapter, we cover:

> - Introduction.
> - Changes in 1994/95 for firms which are assessed on the PY basis.
> - Changes between 6 April 1995 and 5 April 1997.
> - Changes for firms who are on the CY basis.
> - Changes after 5 April 1997.

Introduction

The way in which a change in accounting date will be dealt with depends upon whether the CY basis of assessment has come into effect. For a firm which was in existence at 5 April 1994, and which has a change before 6 April 1996, the position will normally be governed by the Inland Revenue's practice which is set out in booklet IR26 — see Appendix 1 to this chapter.

For a firm which is already on the CY basis, or which moves on to the CY basis from 1997/98, the position is governed by the Finance Act 1994.

Changes in 1994/95 for firms which are assessed on the PY basis

The treatment normally adopted by the Inland Revenue is to assess profits for the year following the tax year in which the accounting date has been changed on the basis of a notional basis period of 12 months ended on the new accounting date in the previous tax year.

29

EXAMPLE

A firm has made up accounts to 30 September for a number of years. In 1995, accounts are made up for a period of nine months to 30 June 1994 and it is intended that 30 June will be the firm's year end from now on. Profits are as follows:

	£
12 months to 30 September 1992	360,000
12 months to 30 September 1993	180,000
9 months to 30 June 1994	120,000

The 1994/95 assessment will normally have been made on £180,000 (preceding year basis).

The 1995/96 assessment will normally be:

	£
$^3/_{12}$ × £180,000 =	45,000
Profits for 9 month period	120,000
	165,000

However, this approach is not adopted where there has been a substantial fluctuation in profits. In such cases, an averaging approach is followed.

EXAMPLE

Ross & Co has made up accounts to 31 March. Its results have been as follows:

	£
Year ended 31 March 1993	60,000
Year ended 31 March 1994	80,000

It changes to a 31 December year end in 1994. Its profits for the nine months ended 31 December 1994 are £32,000.

The assessment for 1995/96 will be computed as follows:

Year ended 31 December 1994

	£
£80,000 × $^3/_{12}$	20,000
1 April 1994 to 31 December 1994	32,000
	52,000

This still leaves 1994/95 which will be dealt with like this:

The total profits for the 33 month combined period are £172,000. This represents a notional figure of £187,636 for a period of three full years (ie $^{36}/_{33}$ × £172,000).

The 1994/95 assessment will then be:

	£	
1993/94	60,000	(PY basis)
1994/95	75,636	
1995/96	52,000	
	187,636	

Changes between 6 April 1995 and 5 April 1997

Where a firm changes its accounting date after 5 April 1995, the position may be slightly different. Unless 1995/96 is assessed on the **actual basis** (in which case 1996/97 will also be assessed on the **actual basis**), the assessment for 1996/97 will be based on a proportion of the profits for a notional period from the end of the 1995/96 basis period until the latest date to which accounts are made up in the tax year 1996/97.

EXAMPLE

A firm has made up accounts to 30 June and so the assessment for 1996/97 will normally be 12/24 x profits for the period 1 July 1994–30 June 1996.

However, if the firm changes its accounting date to 31 March 1997, there will be two accounting periods which end in 1996/97, the year ended 30 June 1996 and the 9 month period 1 July 1996–31 March 1997.

Where there are two periods ending in the same tax year, they are effectively treated as one single period so the 1996/97 assessment will now be determined as 12/33 x profits for the period 1 July 1994–31 March 1997.

Changes for firms who are on the CY basis

A change of accounting date will result in a change of basis period only if certain conditions contained in FA 1994, s 202 are satisfied:

(1) The period from the end of the previous accounting period to the new accounting date must not exceed 18 months.

(2) The change in accounting date must have been notified to an officer of the Board of Inland Revenue on or before the 31 January following the tax year in which the change is made.

(3) Either there must have been no change of basis period in the previous five years or the officer of the Board must be satisfied that the change is made for genuine commercial reasons. These must have been set out in writing in the notification mentioned in (2) above.

Provided that these conditions are satisfied, the treatment depends upon whether the new accounting date is less or more than 12 months after the last set of accounts ended (FA 1994, s 201).

Where the new accounting date is less than 12 months after the previous accounting date, the legislation requires the assessment to be made for a notional period of 12 months ending with the new accounting date.

EXAMPLE

A firm which is assessed on the CY basis has made up accounts to 30 April. It decides to make up accounts to 31 March and accounts are prepared for an 11 month period ended 31 March 1998.

The assessable profits for 1997/98 will be ascertained as follows:

$\frac{1}{12}$ × profits for year ended 30 April 1997 **plus** profits for 11 months ended 31 March 1998.

Where the period is for more than 12 months, the assessable profits for the year in which the new accounting date falls will normally be the full amount of those profits, as reduced by any **overlap relief**.

EXAMPLE

A firm with 31 March year end draws up accounts for an 18 month period ended 30 September 1998.

The 1998/99 assessment will be on the full amount of the profits for that 18 month period, subject to a deduction for overlap relief.

In a case such as the above, there may be one tax year in which no period of account ends (in the example, this is the case for 1997/98). The assessment for the year will normally be made on the **fiscal year basis**.

Appendix 1 — Extract from IR26 on change of accounting date

1. This sets out briefly the practice of the Board of Inland Revenue in cases where a trader permanently changes his accounting date.

Statutory provisions

2. The relevant statutory provisions are contained in ICTA 1988, s 60. The effect of these provisions is briefly as follows:

    (i) In the normal case where there is only one account ending in the year preceding the year of assessment and that account is for a period of one year, the assessment is to be based on the profit of that account (ICTA 1988, s 60(3)).

    (ii) In other cases, the Board of Inland Revenue are to decide what period of 12 months ending on a date in the preceding Income Tax year is to be the basis year (ICTA 1988, s 60(4)). There is no appeal against that decision.

    (iii) Where the Board have determined the basis year for any Income Tax year under (ii), they may direct the

CHANGES IN ACCOUNTING PERIODS

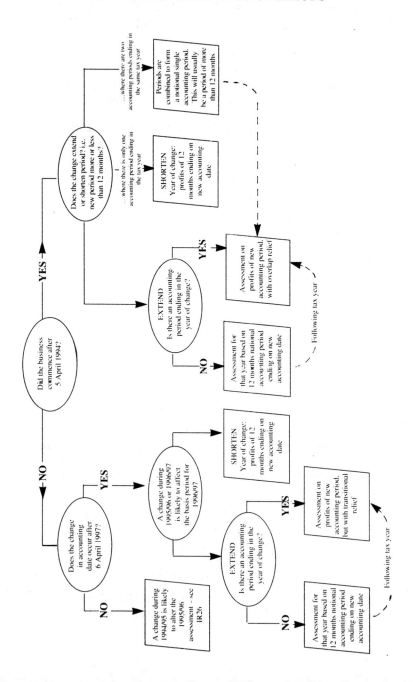

assessment for the preceding Income Tax year is to be adjusted to the profits of the corresponding period, ie the year ending on the same date in the previous year (ICTA 1988, s 60(5)); and appeal against the Board's decision or make or not to make any such direction lies to the General or Special Commissioners, who are empowered to grant 'such relief, if any, as is just'.

Board's normal practice

3.   Under [ICTA 1988 s 60(4)] the Board normally decide that the assessment is to be based on the profits of the period of 12 months ending on the new accounts date in the preceding Income Tax year, ie the date to which the trader proposes to make up his accounts in future.

4.   The question then arises whether there is to be any adjustment of the assessment for the preceding Income Tax year under [ICTA 1988 s 60(5)] to the profits of the 'corresponding' period. Such an adjustment may increase or decrease the liability, according to the trend of profits.

5.   The considerations which the Board have in mind in determining this question are as follows:

Where there is a permanent change of accounting date then, whether or not revision under [ICTA 1988 s 60(5)] is ordered, one of two things must, in the ordinary course, happen;

(*a*) If the new date is later in the Income Tax year than the old, the profits of some period will not come into assessment at all.

(*b*) If the new date is earlier in the Income Tax year than the old, the profits of some period will come into assessment twice.

If the profits of the period omitted were relatively low, or the profits of the period coming in twice were relatively high, the Revenue would gain conversely, if the profits of the period omitted were relatively high, or the profits of the period coming in twice were relatively low, the taxpayer would gain. The Board attempt to secure that the profits to be assessed twice, or to be omitted from assessment, as the case may be, are 'average' profits. As a rule this object can be secured neither by straightforward revision nor by non-revision, but only by taking for the year to which ICTA 1988, s 60(5) applies some figure intermediate between the revised and unrevised figures, and it is the Board's normal practice to propose, subject to the concurrence of the Commissioners of Income Tax having jurisdiction in the particular case, the adoption of such an intermediate figure. That intermediate figure is computed by reference to a consideration of:

(i) the profits of all the accounting periods of which any part enters into either the year (or, in some cases, years) under ICTA 1988, s 60(4) or the 'corresponding period' under [ICTA 1988, s 60(5)] [referred to subsequently as the 'relevant accounting periods'], and

(ii) the number of years for which the assessments are based in whole or in part on any of the profits of the 'relevant accounting periods' [referred to subsequently as the 'relevant years'].

The profits of the 'relevant accounting periods' are expanded or reduced on a time basis so as to give a proportionate figure [referred to subsequently as the 'aggregate profit'] for the 'relevant years', and the assessment for the year to which s 60(5) applies is adjusted, up or down as the case may be, so that the total of the assessments for all the 'relevant years' is precisely equal to the 'aggregate profit'.

Right of Appeal

6.   It is open to the taxpayer, if he does not accept the Board's proposal, to appeal to the General or Special Commissioners against any direction by the Board that may be made under s 60(5) or against a decision not to issue a direction, and the Commissioners are empowered on appeal to give such relief, if any, as is just. The Board's proposal represents the solution which they consider would be likely to commend itself to the Commissioners and where it is accepted there

is in effect an agreed recommendation as to what is thought to be just.

Special cases

7. The practice outlined above is suitable for the majority of cases. There are, however, certain classes of case which are incapable of solution along these lines for which modifications are necessary, eg:

(*a*) cases where the 'aggregate profit' is not intermediate between the sum of the assessments for the 'relevant years' without revision under s 60(5) and the sum of the assessments for those years after revision under that section;

(*b*) cases where there is a marked seasonal fluctuation in the rate of profit (eg as in the case of the seaside hotel);

(*c*) cases where in some or all of the periods concerned losses were incurred;

(*d*) cases where any one of the years concerned is affected by the commencement or cessation provisions.

The modifications that are introduced to deal with these special types of case cannot be described in detail within the limits of the leaflet, but the general method followed throughout is that of equating the average rate of assessments over the years affected to the average rate of profits in the accounting periods that form the basis of those assessments.

Small differences

8. Where the 'average' computation brings out an 'aggregate profit' which exceeds, or falls short of, the sum of the unrevised assessment for the preceding year and the assessments for the other 'relevant years' a relatively small amount, it is not the Board's normal practice to take any action by way of 'average' adjustment. For this purpose, the Board would normally regard as relatively small a difference that was less than ten per cent of the average of the current and preceding years' assessments and also less than £1,000.

Chapter 4

Tax planning and anti-avoidance provisions

This chapter concentrates mainly on firms which were already in existence at 5 April 1994 and which have been on the preceding year basis of assessment (see Chapter 3).

We examine the following:

- Planning in relation to the basis period for 1995/96
- Transitional year basis period.
- Basis of assessment for 1997/98.
- Firms on the actual basis for 1995/96.
- Anti-avoidance provisions.
- Summary of possible opportunities for tax savings.

Planning in relation to the basis period for 1995/96

If your firm is on the PY basis, the assessment for 1995/96 will be based on your profits for an accounting year which falls in 1994/95. All other things being equal (which, of course, they seldom are), the general advice has been that firms should try to keep profits for this period as low as possible, and defer recognition of income until the **transitional year basis period** as only 50 per cent of the profits for that period will be taxed.

EXAMPLE

Graham and Martin make up their accounts to 30 November. They are at present taxed on the PY basis.

Their management accounts for the nine months ended 31 August 1994 forecast profits for the year ended 30

November 1994 of £200,000 and a budget for the coming year of £240,000. However, this is on the basis of the following assumptions:
— a general provision against bad debts (in fact there are two fees currently outstanding which are more than six months old and which add up to £28,000);
— budgeted costs of £14,000 for various consultancy work which the firm needs to have done by 31 December 1994;
— consultancy fees of £10,000 per annum payable to former partners;
— staff bonuses for 1993/94 of £23,000;
— estimated annual contribution towards staff pension scheme of £17,000;
— rent due to Graham of £16,000 per annum payable on the normal quarter days.

Subject to the anti-avoidance provisions (see below), there may be scope for minimising the 1995/96 assessment by taking the following steps:

i)   make a specific bad debts provision. This means that the £28,000 should be an allowable deduction in arriving at taxable profits for the year ended 30 November 1994;
ii) arrange for the consultancy work to be started before 30 November 1994 and for invoices to be rendered by that date — this should secure a deduction in the accounts for the year ended 30 November 1994;
iii) again — arrange for the former partners to bill before 30 November 1994;
iv) ensure that the staff bonuses are actually paid by 31 August 1995 (nine months after the year end) so that a deduction is due for the year ended 30 November 1994;
v)   make sure that the pension contributions are actually paid by 30 November 1994 — otherwise they will be allowed only as and when they are paid. It may also be possible to pay the next year's contribution in advance.

The net effect could be as follows:

	Year ended 30 November 1994 (taxable 1995/96)	Year ended 30 November 1995 (only 50% taxable)
	£	£
Forecast/budget	200,000	240,000
deduct:		
consultancy	(14,000)———	14,000
former partners fees	(10,000)———	10,000
1994/95 staff pension		
contribution paid in advance	(17,000)———	17,000
	159,000	281,000

The total profits for the two years remain the same, but by making these changes the firm may be able to reduce the 1995/96 tax assessment by £41,000 at the expense of paying tax on additional taxable income for 1996/97 of £20,500.

Furthermore, it may be possible to vary the partnership agreement and the terms of the lease so that Graham receives a prior allocation of profits in the place of rent. This will mean that the profits of the transitional year basis period will be increased (but only 50 per cent will be assessed). Instead of paying tax on Schedule A income of £16,000 per annum, Graham will pay tax on a correspondingly increased share of partnership profits.

The changed arrangements may save Schedule A assessments for two years (1995/96 and 1996/97) on £16,000 per annum in exchange for additional partnership profits of £16,000 assessable for 1996/97.

Transitional year basis period

This term relates to the period, generally 24 months, which is averaged to arrive at the assessable profits for 1996/97 (see Chapter 3 at p 31). Once again, and subject to the anti-avoidance provisions, it will pay most firms to recognise as much income during this period as possible.

EXAMPLE

Dorothy and David make up accounts to 30 April.

Assume that their profits for the year ending 30 April 1995 are £85,000 and they forecast profits of £115,000 for the year ending 30 April 1996.

The firm also has a long-term assignment which, on completion, is likely to give rise to an exceptional profit of £40,000. Also, certain dilapidations will need to be made good at some time over the next two to three years at an estimated cost of £20,000.

Once again, it would be 'tax efficient' if the long-term assignment could be completed within the year ending 30 April 1996 or (if this is not possible) for the client to make a substantial payment on account. Conversely, from a tax planning standpoint the dilapidation work should not be actually put in hand until after the end of the transitional basis period.

The ideal position would be as follows:

	Assessable 1996/97	Allowable in full in a later year
	£	£
Profit on long term assignment	40,000	
Dilapidations		(20,000)
'Normal' profits:		
Year ended 30 April 1995	85,000	
Year ended 30 April 1996	115,000	
	240,000	
Assessable 1996/97 (50%)	120,000	
Allowable in a later year		(20,000)

Compared with the worst case position

	Assessable 1996/97	Assessable in full in a later year
	£	£
Dilapidations	(20,000)	
Profit on longer term assignment		40,000
'Normal' profits:		
Year ended 30 April 1995	85,000	
Year ended 30 April 1996	115,000	
	180,000	
Assessable 1996/97 (50%)	90,000	
		40,000

It may pay to extend your firm's accounting period

In some situations, the firm may expect to receive an exceptional recept in 1996/97, but after the end of the transitional year basis period. It could be appropriate to extend the firm's accounting date or to have two sets of accounts drawn up in 1996/97.

EXAMPLE

Colin and Bernard normally make up accounts to 31 May. If they also had accounts drawn up for the period of ten months from 1 June 1996–31 March 1997, their transitional year basis period would be the extended period of 34 months from 1 June 1994–31 March 1997, and the assessment for 1996/97 would be based on 12/34 of the profits for that period.

Basis of assessment for 1997/98

There are situations in which it could be beneficial if income arose in the transitional relief period which ends during the tax year 1997/98 rather than in the transitional year basis period. The potential benefit arises because transitional relief is available as a deduction for the tax year in which the individual leaves the firm. So if you are retiring in 1997/98, or indeed at some point in the following three or four years, bear in mind the following example:

EXAMPLE

Colin is aged 59 and is due to retire on 31 May 1999.

The firm's projected profits are as follows:

	£
Year ended 31 May 1995	140,000
Year ended 31 May 1996	135,000
10 months ended 31 March 1997	235,000
2 months ended 31 May 1997	20,000
10 months ended 31 March 1998	130,000

As we have seen from the previous example, the firm could take advantage of the transitional year basis period by having accounts drawn up to 31 March 1997, and the 1996/97 assessment would then be made on profits of £180,000 (ie $\frac{12}{34}$ × aggregate profits of £510,000 for the period 1 June 1994–31 March 1997).

On the other hand, if the firm kept its 31 May year end, the 1996/97 assessment would be arrived at as $\frac{12}{24}$ × £275,000 (two years ended 31 May 1997) ie £137,500. The profits assessable for 1997/98 would then be £255,000 (ie profits for the 12 months ended on 31 May 1997).

At first sight, moving the accounting date to 31 March 1997 is most beneficial. However, when Colin retires his transitional relief will be affected by the decision taken on this. The total transitional relief will be either:

	£
(year end kept at 31 May) $\frac{10}{12}$ × £225,000 ie	187,500

or (if accounts are made up to 31 March 1997) $\frac{5}{365}$ × profits for the year ended 31 March 1998 — 2,055

There is no substitute for making detailed comparisons, and what may suit one partner may not be ideal for another.

Firms on the actual basis for 1995/96

Many of the above complications fall away if your firm is assessed on the actual basis for 1995/96. As we have explained in Chapter 2, this could come about because you and your partners collectively chose to have a cessation on a change in partners between 6 April 1992 and 5 April 1994. It would also happen because your firm started business in 1993/94 and you have chosen to have your profits for the second and third tax years assessed on the actual basis (see p 15).

The basic rule is that where a firm is assessed on the actual basis for 1995/96, the same will apply to 1996/97. Thus, suppose that you have a 30 April year end, if your 1995/96 assessment is arrived at on the actual basis, the 1996/97 assessment will be determined as follows:

$$\tfrac{25}{365} \times \text{profits for the year ended 30 April 1996}$$

$$\textbf{plus } \tfrac{340}{365} \times \text{profits for the year ended 30 April 1997.}$$

On the other hand, when you retire (or change your accounting date) you should be entitled to transitional relief based on $\tfrac{340}{365}$ × the profits for the year ended 30 April 1997.

Anti-avoidance provisions

It has not escaped the Revenue that professional firms might endeavour to capitalise on the transitional rules, by shifting income into the basis period for 1996/97 (the 'transitional year basis period') as only a proportion (normally $\tfrac{12}{24}$ths) of such income will be taxed.

Accordingly, a *Press Release* was issued on 31 March 1994 (see Appendix 1) which stated that anti-avoidance rules will be introduced which will cancel any tax advantages that might accrue from artificial movements of profits into periods of account that form the transitional basis period or the transitional relief period.

The anti-avoidance rules will refer to 'triggers'. These will be transactions, events or changes in practice which may bring the partners within the scope of the anti-avoidance rules. The specified triggers are:

- Changes in accounting policy;
- Transactions with connected persons;

- 'Self cancelling' transactions or arrangements involving unconnected persons, eg the sale of stock immediately before the end of the transitional basis period and its repurchase on the first day of the next accounting period;
- Changes in business behaviour such as any change in a 'settled practice' as to the timing of the supply of goods or services, invoicing, collection of debts, incurring of business expenses, payments on account and settlement of outstanding debts.

The tax savings which could otherwise be achieved will be prevented by a counteracting adjustment unless the firm can show that the triggers happened because of bona fide commercial reasons, the burden of proof being on the taxpayer.

In fact, **the end result could be worse than if no attempt were made to shift profits into the transitional year basis period**. In a worked example in the Revenue's *Press Release*, an attempt to shift £5,000 profits into the two year period ending in 1996/97 results in tax being levied on £7,500. This arises because the profits which have shifted into the transitional year basis period remain assessable for that year even though a counteracting adjustment is made for the year in which the profits properly belong.

Partnership borrowings

The Revenue have identified another potential loophole. Where a firm pays overdraft interest, it is treated like any other expense. This means that interest which is paid during the transitional year basis period will not be relieved in full: if the 1996/97 assessment is based on 12/24ths of the profits for the two years ended 30 April 1996, only half of the interest paid in the period will be effectively relieved.

There is another route under which partners may secure relief for interest on a loan used to finance the firm's business. If partners raise personal loans, and use the borrowed money to subscribe for partnership capital, the interest is allowed as a charge against the partners' personal income.

It has, therefore, been suggested that partners should raise personal loans to replace the firm's 'core' overdraft, with a view to securing relief for all the interest paid in the transitional year basis period.

The Government, therefore, intends to counteract any tax saving unless there are bona fide commercial reasons for refinancing the firm in this way. However, the *Press Release* makes it clear that the proposed legislation will not apply to any re-financing arrangements completed before 31 March 1994, nor will it apply if the firm is assessed on an actual basis for 1996/97.

Other income

Broadly similar rules will apply to income tax under Cases III to V of Schedule D which is artificially moved into the transitional period.

Summary of possible opportunities for tax saving

The most appropriate strategy for a firm must depend upon the particular circumstances of the case such as the pattern of profits, likelihood of partners retiring in the medium term and many other aspects. Inevitably, therefore, we can do no more than suggest possible ways of taking full advantage of the transitional rules and the following is a check-list of points to be considered.

Should your firm have a cessation before 5 April 1997?

- Will there be an opportunity to achieve this because partners are joining or leaving the firm? Can this opportunity be engineered, eg by an equity partner becoming a salaried partner or vice versa?
- Will there be a problem because of the Revenue's right under the existing legislation to adjust the tax assessments for the two years prior to the year of cessation to an actual basis?
- Precisely when is the optimum date for a cessation?
- Is it important to you that you cease to have joint and several liability for tax liabilities of the firm?

Will the tax assessment for 1996/97 be based on a proportion of the profits for the transitional year basis period?

If so:

- Are there likely to be any exceptional profits during the period? If so, the tax treatment can be beneficial since only half of such profits will normally be taxed.

- It may make better sense to purchase equipment rather than lease it, since relief will effectively be obtained only for 50 per cent of rentals which refer to the transitional year basis period. In contrast, capital allowances provide full relief since it is profits before capital allowances which are averaged.

- Should you consider advancing salaried partners to equity partner status so that they will share in the 1996/97 assessment? In some cases the tax benefits may be increased if they also share in the 1995/96 assessment. Clearly, however, there are wider issues involved in advancing salaried partners.

- Can partners introduce any personal capital so as to reduce borrowings and maximise profits for one of the two years falling within the transitional year basis period?

- Are the premises from which the firm's business is carried on owned by one of the partners? If so, there may be tax benefits from changing the position so that the partner receives a prior share of profits rather than rent.

- Could there be an advantage in extending the firm's accounts for 1997 to a date such as 31 March 1997? This may mean that the assessment for 1996/97 will be arrived at as 12/35 of the profits of a 35 month period ending 31 March 1997 rather than 12/24 of the profits for a 24 month period. Your finance partner needs to sit down with your accountants and run through 'what if?' calculations which show the likely consequences of a changed accounting date.

- Can your firm organise matters so that former partners receive annuities rather than consultancy fees? Annuities are allowed as a charge against profits, and this means that there is no question of averaging annuity payments made during the transitional year basis period.

- Are some of your partners due to retire during the two years ending 5 April 1999? If so, make sure that the firm will not have a cessation which enables the Revenue to adjust the 1996/97 assessment to actual (it will normally be possible to avoid this provided there is at least one continuing partner).

Can you make out a commercial case for re-financing your firm?

- There may be good commercial reasons for partners taking personal loans to put in partnership capital. If so, it may be possible to obtain relief for all the interest paid during the transitional year basis period rather than only a proportion as will be the case where the borrowings are taken by the firm itself.

• Can you raise loans where there is an initial 'holiday', with interest payable only after 5 April 1997? At present, it seems that such interest on loans may be outside the proposed anti-avoidance rules.

Appendix 1 — Extracts from Inland Revenue Press Release of 31 March 1994

Self-employed trades, professions and vocations (including partnerships)

1. At present income taxed under Schedule D is assessed on a preceding year basis except in the first and last years of trading. Under the rules in the 1994 Finance Bill, such income will from 1997/98 be taxed on a current year basis. Businesses commencing after 5 April 1994 or deemed to commence under s 113(1) ICTA 1988 following a change after that date in the membership of a partnership will be immediately taxed on the new current year basis.

2. 1996/97 will be a transitional year for which the rules for computation are set out in the 1994 Finance Bill, Sched 19 [now FA 1994, Sched 20]. Tax for this year will normally be assessed on the profits from the end of the 1995/96 basis period (the accounting date ending in 1994/95) to the latest accounting date ending in 1996/97 (the 'transitional period'). In the normal case that will be a 24 month period, and one half of the profits will be taxed. In cases where the accounting date is changed, the period may be longer or shorter.

3. Under the new rules, the 1997/98 assessment will normally be based on the 12 months accounts ending in that year. That proportion of the profits which arises before 5 April 1997 will be available as transitional relief for deduction from the profits of the final period of trading, or, if earlier, when the accounting date of the business moves to 5 April. This means that eventually the profits arising in the period

immediately preceding 5 April 1997 (the 'transitional relief period') will drop out of account.

4. The proposed provisions will cancel any tax advantage that might accrue from artificial movement of profits into periods of account that form the transitional basis period or the transitional relief period. In certain circumstances such counteraction will extend to taxing in full, as well as in a proportionate amount, profits which are artificially moved into the 1996/97 period. Similarly, the amount of transitional relief may be reduced by the full amount of the profits shifted into the basis period for 1997/98 of which the transitional relief period forms a part.

5. In some circumstances, businesses will be taxed for 1996/97 on the actual profits arising in the year to 5 April 1997. Such businesses will not be affected by the proposed provisions set out in this Press Release.

Proposals identifying the avoidance and cancelling the benefit

6. The legislation will take a four-step approach. The first step is to identify the type of transaction, event or change in practice — referred to collectively as 'triggers' — which may bring taxpayers within the scope of the anti-avoidance rules. Those triggers are:

    — a change of one accounting policy for another or a modification within one policy;

    — transactions with persons with whom the taxpayer has some family or proprietorial link (typically 'connected' persons) including partnerships;

    — arrangements with unconnected persons which are wholly or partly reciprocal or self-cancelling, for example the sale of stock immediately before the end of the transitional basis period and re-purchase immediately afterwards;

    — changes in business behaviour, which need not involve any changes in accounting policy. This would mean any change in a settled practice of a trade, profession or vocation as to the timing of any of the following:

> — on the incoming side of a business the supply of goods or services, the invoicing of customers or clients and the collection of debts (including payments on account);
>
> — on the expenditure side of a business the obtaining of goods or services, the incurring of business expenses and the settlement of outstanding debts (including making payments on account).

7. Any case that falls into one of these four categories will be treated as raising a prima facie case for challenge that avoidance has taken place unless either:

   a) the obtaining of a tax advantage arising from an increase in the profits of the transitional basis period, or as the case may be of the transitional relief period, is not the main benefit or one of the main benefits that can reasonably be expected to arise from the trigger, or

   b) the business can show that the triggering transaction was undertaken solely for bona fide commercial reasons. Obtaining a tax advantage will not be such a reason; or,

   c) the absolute and relative amounts of profits shifted into particular periods fall below a prescribed limit, or the turnover of the business is less than a prescribed amount. The legislation will provide powers to make Regulations to set these amounts which will be announced by 5 April 1997. The Government's intention is to deter people from undertaking triggering transactions; it is therefore not appropriate at this stage to indicate the level at which these limits will be set.

8. If the business is not excluded by any one of the tests in para 7 above, the increase in profits identified for the transitional basis period will be charged in full in addition to the profits averaged down, without any adjustments to the profits for any other year of assessment. For the transitional relief period, the transitional relief will be reduced by the full amount of the profits moved into the basis period for 1997/98. The effect is demonstrated in

Examples 1 and 2 respectively in the Annex [reproduced below].

Interest paid

14. Payments of interest on borrowings to finance a trade or profession carried on in partnership may presently be relieved in one of two ways. Either there can be a deduction in the partnership accounts, if the interest is paid by the partnership on a partnership loan, or individual partners can get a deduction under ICTA 1988, s 353 for their own borrowings used to finance the partnership. For the transitional year 1996/97 partnerships choosing the first method would get relief only on a proportion of the interest paid, corresponding to the fraction applied to the basis period for that year. But if they claimed relief under s 353 the partners would be eligible for relief on the full amount of interest paid on a fiscal year basis. The Revenue are aware that partnerships are being advised to obtain new personal loans to ensure they get relief under s 353.

15. The Government intends to legislate to ensure that, unless there are bona fide commercial reasons for the re-financing and the main or one of the main purposes is not to obtain a tax advantage, ICTA 1988, s 353 relief will be reduced proportionately. Any interest which qualifies for relief under s 353 and is paid in the period between the end of the 1995/96 basis period and 6 April 1997 (exclusive) will be reduced to the fraction of which the numerator is 12 and the denominator the number of months in that period. The effect of these proposals is shown in Example 3 in the Annex [reproduced below]. They will not apply to any re-financing arrangements completed before 31 March 1994.

ANNEX

EXAMPLE 1

Transitional basis period avoidance (para 8)

Geoffrey returns profits as follows:

Year ended 5 April 1995	£10,000
2 years ended 5 April 1997	£30,000

The assessments are:

1995/96		£10,000
1996/97	£30,000 × $^{12}/_{24}$ =	£15,000

Profits of £5,000 were shifted from the year ended 5 April 1995 to the following period by means of one of the triggers. If Geoffrey is unable to demonstrate that either of the exclusions in para 7(*a*) or (*b*) applies, £5,000 will be added to the returned assessment for 1996/97, making £20,000 in all. The assessment for 1995/96 will remain unchanged.

EXAMPLE 2

Transitional relief period avoidance (para 8)

Helen returns profits as follows:

Year ended 5 October 1997	£36,000
Year ended 5 October 1998	£24,000

The assessments are:

1997/98	£36,000
1998/99	£24,000

Transitional relief in respect of the apportioned profits for the period from 6 October 1996 to 5 April 1997 would be £36,000 × $^{6}/_{12}$ = £18,000.

Profits of £6,000 were shifted from the year ended 5 October 1998 to the previous year by means of one of the triggers. If Helen is unable to demonstrate that either of the exclusions in para 7(a) or (b) applies, the transitional relief will be reduced by £6,000 to £12,000. There will be no further adjustments.

EXAMPLE 3

Refinancing of partnership borrowing (para 15)

Ian is a partner in ABC & Co which draws up accounts to 5 April. In 1994/95, he borrows £100,000 and introduces it into the partnership to reduce the partnership overdraft. In each of the years 1995/96 and 1996/97 he pays interest of £7,500, for which he claims relief under ICTA 1988, s 353. He is unable to demonstrate that the re-financing is undertaken for bona fide commercial reasons. The relief is reduced in the ratio 12/24: he is given relief of £3,750 in each of these years.

Janet is a partner in DE & Co which draws up accounts to 5 May. On 6 May 1994, she borrows £240,000 and introduces it into DE & Co to enable a term loan to be paid off early. In 1994/95 she pays interest of £16,500, and in each of the years 1995/96 and 1996/97 interest of £18,000. She claims relief each year under s 353. She is unable to demonstrate that the refinancing is undertaken for bona fide commercial reasons. The relief is reduced in the ratio 12/35 ie an average 12-month measure of interest paid is spread over the entire period from the start of the transitional basis period (6 May 1994) to the end of the transitional relief period (5 April 1997). This is to ensure that some relief is given for 1996/97. She is given relief of £5,658 in 1994/95 and £6,172 in both 1995/96 and 1996/97.

Chapter 5

Self assessment from 1996/97 — how this will affect solicitors

In this chapter, we cover the following:

OUTLINE OF THE NEW SYSTEM

- Background.
- Liability to make self-assessments.
- Inclusion of estimates.
- Amendments to a self-assessment after it has been filed.
- Revenue enquiries and right to audit.
- Requirement to notify chargeability.

PAYMENT OF TAX AND 'INCENTIVES' TO COMPLY

- Payment of tax.
- Surcharges.
- Interest and penalties.

PARTNERSHIPS

- Partners' obligations to make returns.
- Inland Revenue investigations into partnership returns.
- Partnership returns.

ACHIEVING FINALITY

- Disclosure.
- Post transaction rulings.

HOW THE SYSTEM WILL OPERATE IN 1996/97

- Transitional rule for investment income.
- Partnerships.

OUTLINE OF THE NEW SYSTEM

Background

The changes which are due to take place in 1997 amount to a fundamental change to the tax system which will change the present set of obligations owed to the Inland Revenue by taxpayers and their advisers. The Revenue will no longer need to initiate proceedings by issuing an assessment, liability for tax will arise automatically.

Under the new regime, taxpayers (or their advisors) will be required to submit tax returns which incorporate a calculation of the tax to be paid (or in some cases, tax to be repaid) and payment of the amount due. In effect, instead of being required to deliver a return, the legislation will require taxpayers to make a self-assessment. This will make life easier, both for taxpayers and the Inland Revenue, since it will replace the present situation where a taxpayer is sent several different assessments on different sources of income and capital gains. Furthermore, there should be a significant reduction in paperwork because the Revenue will no longer have to issue estimated assessments and amended assessments.

The return will be capable of being processed by computerised scanning equipment, which will further reduce the clerical work required at the Revenue's offices.

Liability to make self-assessments

Any person served with a notice by an Officer of the Board of Inland Revenue (from now on he or she will simply be known as the 'Officer') must file a return. Normally, the filing date will be 31 January following the end of the tax year. However, if the Officer is late in serving notice on an individual for him to make a self-assessment, the **filing date** may be extended. Basically, the Officer must give the individual at least three months to make the self-assessment. Thus, if the notice requiring the delivery of a self-assessment is served after 31 October, it does not need to be delivered to the Inland Revenue until three months later.

Alternative to self-assessment

Provided a return of income and chargeable gains is delivered to the Revenue not later than 30 September following the end of the tax year, the Inland Revenue will calculate the amount of tax payable and issue an assessment.

If the Officer is late in issuing the notice to make a self-assessment, the 30 September deadline may be extended. Basically, the taxpayer will be given at least two months in which to complete and deliver the return and so if the Officer serves the notice after 31 July the deadline for filing the return will be later than the normal 30 September deadline.

The Revenue have confirmed that if they receive a return by 30 September, but do not issue a notice of the tax payable by 31 December, the trigger date for interest and surcharge will be 30 days after the issue of the statement of tax which is payable.

Inclusion of estimates

The Revenue have stated their intention that if a taxpayer includes an estimate in his return, the rest of the return will become final within the normal timescale provided it is completed to the best of the taxpayer's knowledge and belief. The Revenue stated that the estimate should be corrected as soon as the missing information is reasonably available, in accordance with, TMA 1970 s 97.

The need for estimates will often arise in relation to capital gains tax (eg valuations at 31 March 1982). It should be borne in mind that a valuation will not be treated as an estimate, unless designated as such by the taxpayer. On the other hand, not all valuations will be estimates, although they may be subject to dispute. The Revenue have agreed that where no enquiry into a valuation is made within 12 months and the valuation falls within the range of bona fide valuations which could arise between valuers who were fully instructed on the facts, they will not be able to re-open the position.

Submission of supporting documents with the self-assessment

The notice which the Officer will send asking for the self-assessment may specify that certain accounts, statements and documents relating to information in the return should be filed at the same time. The Inland Revenue will certainly continue to require business accounts for a sole practitioner or a partnership. Other documents which may be required will include books, contracts, deeds, receipts etc.

The legislation specifies that records must be retained for a minimum period after the submission of the self-assessment, in case they are required by the Officer. Personal records must be retained for 12 months after the filing date. Business records must normally be retained for a minimum period of five years after the filing date.

The Finance Act 1994 also sets out the business records which should be retained for examination. The following need to be retained:

- Records of all amounts received and expended in the course of the trade or profession, and the matters in respect of which the receipts and expenditure took place;
- All supporting documents relating to such items.

This requirement is, of course, extremely wide and general in nature. The one positive aspect is that the Taxes Management Act has been amended to make it clear that the taxpayer will be protected if he has preserved information in such a way that original documents can be reproduced. This means that a microfilming system will be as acceptable as the retention of the original documents. Moreover, the Revenue are expected to publish a guidance note on what records should be retained. Mr Stephen Dorrell, Financial Secretary to the Treasury, stated during the Standing Committee debate:

> Guidance will be issued so that the taxpayer can be clear about what sort of records to keep to discharge the new duty. It will not be necessary for him to keep every piece of paper that has ever been connected with his income. It is important both for the taxpayer and the Revenue to focus on the papers that give clear and useful information.

A penalty of up to £3,000 can be imposed for failure to keep records.

Amendments to a self-assessment after it has been filed

A notice may be given to the Inland Revenue amending the self-assessment. This notice may be given within 12 months of the filing date (ie 31 January or three months after the Officer gives notice asking for the self-assessment, whichever is the later).

The Inland Revenue may also amend the self-assessment within nine months of receiving it in order to correct obvious errors of principle, arithmetical errors and the like (this is called 'repairing' a self-assessment).

Revenue enquiries and right to audit

The Inland Revenue may start an enquiry into a self-assessment (or, where the taxpayer has filed an amendment, into the amended self-assessment).

However, the Officer must give written notice of his intention to make an enquiry. Furthermore, that notice must be served within a strict time limit ie:

- 12 months after the date that the self-assessment was delivered; or
- Where the self-assessment is delivered after the filing date, the quarter date following 12 months after delivery. For this purpose, the quarter dates are 31 January, 30 April, 31 July and 31 October. Thus, if a self-assessment which is due on 31 January is not in fact delivered until 31 March, the time limit for the Revenue starting an enquiry expires on 30 April of the following year.

It should also be noted that the Inland Revenue will not be allowed to institute more than one enquiry during the time limit. Once a return or an amendment has been subject to enquiry, no further notice may be given.

Once a notice of intention to enquire has been issued, the Officer may issue a notice requiring the production of documents which are in the possession or power of the person on whom the notice has been served. These must be documents etc which are reasonably required by the Officer to determine to what extent, if at all, the self-assessment or amendment is incorrect.

The notice may also require accounts or other particulars which he may reasonably require. The notice must give a time limit for the production of the documents etc and the taxpayer must be allowed at least 30 days to produce the documents.

An appeal may be made to the Commissioners against a notice. They can either set the notice aside if they think that it is invalid or confirm its validity. If the Commissioners decide that the notice is valid, the documents must be produced within 30 days of the Commissioner's decision. Continued failure to comply may result in a penalty of up to £150 per day.

There is no specified time limit in which an enquiry must be completed. During the Committee stage debate, the Financial Secretary stated a code of practice will be issued on the conduct of enquiries. One aspect to be covered in the code will be the requirement on the Revenue for it to proceed with reasonable speed once it has launched an enquiry and not to drag the process out unnecessarily. The code of practice will set the ground rules which will apply to Revenue Offices when they conduct an enquiry.

In response to a suggestion that the Revenue should have less time in which to initiate an enquiry, the Financial Secretary said that there would then be a risk of precipitating an enquiry into a case for which information would later become available that would render that enquiry unnecessary. If an Officer has not notified his conclusion the taxpayer may, of course, ask the Commissioners to direct the Officer to issue a notice of his conclusions. The Commissioners are required to make such a direction unless they are satisfied that the Officer has reasonable grounds for continuing with the enquiry.

Once the Officer who is conducting the enquiry has completed his investigation, he must say so and state his conclusions as to the correct amount of tax which should be in the self-assessment.

Correction of self-assessments

There are provisions for the self-assessment to be amended by the taxpayer in accordance with the conclusions notified by the Officer conducting the enquiry. However, if the taxpayer does not correct the self-assessment in accordance with the Officer's conclusions, the Officer will issue a notice of amendment (in effect an assessment) against which an appeal may be made within 30 days. If the dispute cannot be settled by agreement, the Commissioners will adjudicate.

Requirement to notify chargeability

The legislation which existed before FA 1994 already imposed an obligation for a person to notify chargeability where the person has not received a return. This must be done within six months of the end of the year of assessment concerned.

PAYMENT OF TAX AND 'INCENTIVES' TO COMPLY

Payment of tax

An individual is required to pay two equal amounts on account of income tax, on 31 January during the year of assessment and on 31 July following the end of the tax year. The amount of the tax payable in this way will normally be equal to the total income tax assessed for the previous year. However, it will be open to a taxpayer (or his advisor) to make a claim before 31 January (ie the normal filing date) for the payments on account to be reduced to 50 per cent of the tax believed to be payable for the year. The Inland Revenue will generally require an explanation for why it is believed that the tax payable will be less than that for the previous year.

When the self-assessment is delivered on the following 31 January, any difference between the payments on account already made and the amount shown as payable for the year will need to be settled. At the same time, it will be necessary to make a payment equal to the capital gains tax liability for the year concerned.

Amended self-assessments

Tax is payable or repayable on the later of:

- 31 January following the end of the tax year; and
- 30 days from the date on which the amendment to the self-assessment was given.

In cases where the Inland Revenue discover that a source of income has not been assessed or has been inadequately assessed, the Officer will normally make an assessment and the tax will be payable 30 days after the assessment has been issued.

Surcharges

Where tax is paid more than 28 days after it fell due, there may be a five per cent surcharge levied by the Inland Revenue. This 28 day period applies both to the payments required on 31 January and 31 July and also to tax which is due 30 days after an assessment has been made.

If the tax remains unpaid more than six months after the due date, there is a further five per cent surcharge.

Mr Stephen Dorrell MP, Financial Secretary to the Treasury, stated during the Committee stage of the Finance Bill 1994:

> ... if a taxpayer has an outstanding obligation which is paid late as a result of a bona fide mistake on a self-assessment which that person later corrects [he may be liable for interest]. However, provided that the taxpayer volunteers the information and pays the amount promptly, a surcharge would not be imposed by the Board.

Appeals against the surcharge

It will be possible for the Inland Revenue to mitigate the whole or part of a surcharge where there is a reasonable excuse for the delay. In cases where there is a dispute with the Revenue as to whether there is a reasonable excuse, the Commissioners can be asked to adjudicate. However, the Finance Act 1994 specifically states that inability to pay is not to be regarded as a reasonable excuse.

Interest and penalties

Interest

Interest will be payable for periods up to the date on which payment is made and is in addition to the surcharges referred to above. This interest does not attract any tax relief.

Penalties

A penalty of £100 will be due if the self-assessment is not delivered by the filing date.

The Inland Revenue may then appeal to the Commissioners for a continuing penalty of up to £60 per day. The starting date for this continuing penalty is the day on which the Commissioners direct that it should be imposed. It is avoided if the self-assessment is delivered before the Commissioners make their decision. However, even if no continuing daily penalty is imposed, there is a further £100 penalty if the self-assessment is delivered more than six months after the filing date.

Where the failure continues beyond 12 months the penalty, in addition to anything mentioned above, is a maximum of the tax due as shown in the return.

Penalty determinations may in future attract an interest charge, where the penalties are not paid promptly, as the determination will be treated as if it were an assessment for the purposes of interest charged on late payment of tax.

Appeals

It will be possible to appeal against the determination of a penalty by the Inspector. However, the Commissioners may only set aside the £100 fixed penalties if there is reasonable excuse for the taxpayer not having delivered the return throughout the period it was overdue. Where this condition is not satisfied, the Commissioners are required to confirm the penalties in full.

PARTNERSHIPS

The basic rules are modified to take account of partnerships.

Partners' obligations to make returns

Individual partners will be required to deliver self-assessments. However, the partnership must also make a return (not strictly speaking a self-assessment) if the Revenue serve a notice on the firm. The Revenue may serve a notice on any partner (the 'representative partner').

The notice will ask for delivery of the return together with accounts and such other statements as the Inland Revenue require. The representative partner will be required to make a return and all items relevant to the agreement of profits assessable under Schedule D Case II must be included in that return. It will not be possible for individual partners to claim a deduction for expenses incurred by them and which are not shown in the partnership return.

The notice will require the partnership return to include:

- The names, addresses and tax references of all persons who have been partners at any time during the period covered by the return. Where partners have been in the firm for only part of the year, the precise period must be specified;
- Full details of each partner's entitlement to profits (and losses) from each source of partnership income;
- Particulars of the disposals of partnership assets as if the partnership itself (not the individual partners) were liable to tax on any chargeable gains and details of each partner's share of such capital gains;
- Details of acquisitions of property by the partnership;
- The amount of annual charges borne by each partner (eg annuities paid to former partners or their dependants).

It will be possible for the partnership to amend its return and for the Inland Revenue to amend it after an enquiry.

Inland Revenue investigations into partnership returns

The Inland Revenue will have the power to enquire into partnership returns on the same basis as they may enquire into returns made by individuals. That is to say, a notice must be issued within 12 months of the filing date or, if the return is delivered after the filing date, at the quarter date following 12 months after the delivery date.

A notice served on the partnership is deemed to include similar notices issued to the individual partners to the extent that they have actually delivered self-assessments.

Partnership returns

Each partner will be liable to a £100 penalty if the partnership return is submitted late. This applies to any person who was a partner at any time during the return period. The continuing daily penalties and the six month £100 penalty also apply to each partner.

Appeals against penalty notices imposed on partners

Where penalty determinations have been made so as to impose either the £100 penalty or the continuing daily penalty in respect of two or more partners, appeals may be brought only by the representative partner. He then makes a composite appeal.

Once again, the £100 penalty must stand unless the Commissioners are satisfied that there was a reasonable excuse which applied throughout the period of default.

Incorrect returns

If an incorrect self-assessment is delivered and it is wrong because of negligent or fraudulent conduct, the maximum penalty remains 100 per cent of the tax understated in the self-assessment.

Incorrect partnership returns

A partnership return, which includes accounts and statements, and which is incorrect due to negligent or fraudulent conduct can give rise to a penalty on each partner, with the maximum amount of the penalty being the tax under assessed on him or her.

It will be possible for this penalty to apply even though the individual partner has not completed the partnership return and has not been guilty of negligent or fraudulent conduct. Basically, the conduct of the representative partner who made the partnership return is all that matters.

ACHIEVING FINALITY

It has generally been accepted that any new regime should afford taxpayers the same degree of certainty that liabilities have been finalised as exists at present where an assessment is appealed against, and there is a determination under TMA 1970, s 54.

Disclosure

The legislation specifically provides that the Inland Revenue may make assessments to correct a loss of tax which has been discovered. However, the Act makes it plain that this may not be done where there has been an error or mistake in a return as to the basis of computing a liability but the basis adopted accorded with the practice generally applying at the time.

Furthermore, no discovery assessment may be made where the Inland Revenue could reasonably have been expected to identify the contentious point in the light of the information provided in the self-assessment. Information provided in the two years prior to the year in which the discovery is to be made is also to be taken into account in this regard.

Discovery assessments will therefore be possible only where relevant information has not been put before the Officer dealing with the self-assessment.

Post-transaction rulings

The Inland Revenue recognise the fact that under the self-assessment regime, it will increasingly be necessary to ascertain how a transaction should be dealt with for tax purposes before making a return. There is no firm commitment at present to introduce a statutory system of advance rulings which will be given before a transaction was carried out, it is rather proposed that there should be **post-transaction** rulings. These rulings will be binding on the Inland Revenue, but will not affect the taxpayer's statutory rights to appeal against an assessment.

The Revenue propose that the application for such a ruling would have to include the following:

- The name and tax reference of the taxpayer;
- Full particulars of the transaction or event in question;
- A statement of the issue(s) to be considered;
- Copies of all relevant documents, with the relevant passages identified;
- A statement that to the best of the taxpayer's knowledge and belief the facts as stated were correct and all relevant facts had been disclosed;
- A statement of the specific point(s) of difficulty giving rise to the ruling request;
- A statement of the ruling requested or suggested as appropriate by the applicant;
- Particulars of sections of the Taxes Acts considered to be relevant;
- Particulars of any case law, statements of practice, extra statutory concessions etc considered to be relevant;
- Particulars of any previous discussions or correspondence about the tax treatment of the transaction, or of any similar transaction between the taxpayer and any Revenue office; and, when the taxpayer or his advisors were aware of correspondence on the transaction between any other person and any Revenue office, particulars of that correspondence;

- A statement of the applicant's opinion of the tax consequence of the transaction, along with reasons to the extent that they were capable of being supplied.

HOW THE SYSTEM WILL OPERATE IN 1996/97

Transitional rule for investment income

A special rule will apply for determining the payments on account for 1996/97, which will fall due on 31 January and 31 July 1997. These will be computed as half the total liability for the previous year less any income tax deducted at source, but for this purpose the liability for 1995/96 will be exclusive of higher rate tax on taxed investment income. The tax on this income for 1996/97 will effectively fall due for payment on 31 January 1998 when the individual files his self-assessment for 1996/97 and settles the difference between his actual liability for the year and the amounts paid on account.

On the other hand, the 1996/97 payments on account will not be divided equally. Basically, the tax relating to Schedule A income and Schedule D Case III income will be payable as part of the amount payable on 31 January 1997.

Partnerships

In determining the final payment due for 1996/97 on 31 January 1998, credit will be given for any tax paid by a partnership on a partner's behalf for 1996/97 — as if this was tax deducted at source. This provision will help to smooth over the transition from the partnership paying the tax for 1996/97 (on 1 January and 1 July 1997) to the partner paying his or her own tax by self-assessment for 1996/97, on 31 January 1998.

Part II

Taxable profits and gains

This book is intended to give solicitors who do not specialise in tax a good grasp of their tax treatment in general so that they can look at the changes to the Schedule D basis of assessment in a broader and more practical context.

There are many important aspects of the tax 'system' which will be unaffected by the introduction of the 'new rules' such as the way in which taxable profits are computed and the legislation which determines whether relief is due for certain payments. We also set out the basics on capital gains tax in so far as this tax is likely to impinge on sole practitioners and partnerships.

We also include extracts from key Revenue Statements so that this book can be used as a 'Primer' and a general reference book.

6 Differences between accounts profits and taxable profits.

7 Capital gains tax in relation to the firm.

8 Miscellaneous tax aspects of a solicitor's practice.

Chapter 6

Differences between accounts profits and taxable profits

Many solicitors — and other professional people, including many accountants, find it difficult to relate their tax assessment to their share of profits as shown in the firm's accounts. In fact, some people find it difficult to distinguish between taxable profits and drawings — which are nothing to do with profits as such! The purpose of this chapter is to enable you to reconcile your accounting profit with your tax assessment based on the accounts.

We look at the following aspects:

- Disallowed expenses.
- 'Timing differences'.
- Debtors and valuation of work in progress
- Partners' salaries and/or interest.
- Preceding year basis of assessment.
- Interest payments and annuities to former partners.
- Capital allowances.
- Adjustments between current accounts.

Disallowed expenses

There are many types of expense which are quite properly deducted for accounts purposes, but which are not allowable for tax purposes.

Depreciation

No tax relief is given for depreciation as such, although similar relief may be given on certain assets via the capital allowances system.

In particular, there is no relief for the following:

- Depreciation of a leasehold interest in a building (except in the specific situation where your firm has paid a **premium** to a landlord which has been taxed in his hands under Schedule A or which would have been taxed if the landlord were not exempt);
- Depreciation of capital expenditure on a building;
- Depreciation (or more precisely 'amortisation') of a lump sum paid to a tenant in return for the assignment of his lease;
- Depreciation of fixtures and fittings;
- Amounts written off in respect of goodwill;
- Depreciation of 'plant and machinery' (but see below regarding **capital allowances**).

Business entertainment

Relief is not due unless the entertainment is staff entertainment. Moreover, the term 'business entertainment' is extended for tax purposes to cover the following:

- Gifts to clients.
- Gifts to potential clients.
- Gifts to potential 'introducers' of business.
- Gifts to suppliers.

There is a small let-out for gifts to clients (but not suppliers) of items such as calendars or diaries which are allowable expenses provided the item carries a 'conspicuous advertisement', and costs no more than £10 (actually the £10 limit relates to the cost of items given to any one recipient during the course of the year).

There is one other distinction which may be relevant to a firm of solicitors. In 1985 an Exeter firm, Ashford Sparkes & Harward succeeded in an appeal before the High Court against a Commissioners' decision that no relief was due for expenditure of £938 on the provision of food and drink for partners at the firm's annual weekend conference at a hotel in Salcombe. There are therefore some circumstances in which entertainment expenses can be tax deductible, although this is an exception to the normal rule.

Interest debits and overdrawn capital accounts

Problems can arise where interest is incurred because of the proprietor's drawings. The most obvious example of this is where a sole practitioner's capital account is overdrawn and in such a situation the Revenue usually seek to disallow the appropriate part of the debit for interest in the practice accounts because part of the interest is not incurred wholly and exclusively for the purposes of the business but for the (private) purpose of financing the practitioner's personal expenses.

There is a distinction between this situation and a case involving a partnership where one particular partner's capital account may be overdrawn but in aggregate the partners' capital accounts are in credit. A District Inspector of Taxes stated in correspondence that:

> It is the Board's view where in total, partners' capital accounts remain in credit, that no restriction should be sought as it can reasonably be argued that the partners with overdrawn accounts are borrowing from those whose accounts are in credit.

Lease rentals on expensive cars

Where a proprietor uses a leased car or provides a motor car to an employee and the original cost was £12,000 or more (£8,000 prior to 11 March 1992), part of the lease rentals must be added back as a disallowable expense. The amount disallowed is the following proportion of the lease rental:

$$\tfrac{1}{2} \times \frac{(\text{Cost of car} - £12{,}000)}{\text{Cost of car}} \times \text{lease rentals.}$$

Thus, if a car which cost £16,000 is leased for a rental of £2,400 per annum, the amount disallowed is:

$$\tfrac{1}{2} \times \frac{(£16{,}000 - 12{,}000)}{16{,}000} \times £2{,}400 \text{ ie } £300.$$

This treatment does not apply to maintenance costs included in the lease rentals provided they are identified separately under the terms of the leasing agreement. Such amounts are fully deductible.

Where a partner uses the car partly for business the restriction may be calculated differently. This, if the £16,000 car had been used 70 per cent for business, 30 per cent for private mileage, the disallowance would be as follows:

	£
amount allowable if no private mileage	2,100
disallow 30 per cent private use	630

Legal and professional

Professional costs incurred in connection with tax appeals are not allowable on the grounds that they relate to tax on profits as opposed to being an expense incurred in earning those profits.

Similarly, professional fees incurred in connection with the acquisition or disposal of capital items are usually disallowed.

Subscriptions

Entrance fees to Professional bodies are not deductible but annual subscriptions are allowable.

Solicitor's Benevolent Fund

The Revenue appear to operate a yardstick whereby a contribution may be disallowed in so far as it exceeds £10 for each of the partners and qualified members of staff (and trainee solicitors).

Guarantee payments

A firm of solicitors may give a guarantee for a loan or for the performance of a contract. No particular problems should arise in securing a deduction for sums which have to be paid out in this connection provided the guarantee was a temporary expedient entered into in order to bring a transaction to a conclusion. In other circumstances the Revenue may argue that payments made under a guarantee are in effect capital losses.

Timing differences

General provisions

Some of the above are **permanent** disallowable items, ie there is never going to be tax relief for such expenditure or for amounts charged in the accounts as depreciation or 'wear and tear'. The position is different on general bad debt provisions in that the problem arises because of a difference between the **timing** of an expense being charged in the firm's accounts and its being an allowable expense for tax purposes.

Thus, the firm may quite legitimately draw up its accounts on the basis that any debts which are more than two months old should be presumed to be doubtful debts. However, if this is a general provision (as opposed to a provision against specific debts) the amount charged in the accounts is not allowable and relief is given only when the debts are written off.

The concept of general and specific provisions is equally applicable to other types of expenses, eg dilapidations which become payable at the expiry of a lease of office premises. Whilst it may be commercially desirable to build up a dilapidations fund over a period of years, tax relief will be available only when the amounts payable can be quantified with reasonable accuracy. This condition is often satisfied only after the lease has expired and negotiations have taken place with the landlord.

Pension scheme contributions

There are other possible **timing** differences. For example, no relief is due if your firm's accounts include a provision for contributions to a staff pension scheme which relate to the year, but have not actually been paid by the year end. Tax relief will be due in a later period in which the contribution is actually paid.

Conversely, your firm may actually have paid a contribution which has to be 'spread' over two or more years in arriving at the firm's profits for tax purposes. Basically, an 'abnormal' contribution which exceeds the aggregate 'ordinary' contributions paid by the firm during the year has to be spread as follows:

Amount of abnormal contribution

£25,000–£50,000	2 year spread
£50,000–£100,000	3 year spread
£100,000 +	4 year spread

Thus a £28,000 abnormal contribution would be allowed in full if the firm made ordinary contributions of £28,000. If this condition were not satisfied, relief would be spread to:

£14,000 — year of payment
£14,000 — following year

Staff bonuses

If your firm so decides, it can charge bonuses which, eg are paid after the year end as an expense which has accrued during the year. This is normal commercial accountancy treatment and the tax treatment follows this **provided** the bonus is actually paid within nine months of the year-end. If the bonus is still unpaid after nine months, it is only allowed for tax purposes as an expense of the year in which it is actually paid.

Redundancy

The Inland Revenue's view is that no relief is due for redundancy costs unless the liability has arisen in the year. In practice, this means that relief is given only if the redundancy notices were served by the year end.

PI claims

An area where the Revenue are particularly difficult concerns the deductibility of a reasonable and scientifically calculated provision for sums that a firm may have to pay out in respect of a negligence claim. There is little doubt that a general provision is not allowed but the Revenue's approach goes beyond this — in essence, the Revenue are firmly of the opinion that a provision is allowable for tax only if the firm has admitted liability. This is a controversial interpretation — and often unrealistic since the firm will often be prevented from conceding that it is liable by the terms of its PI insurance. However, in practice the professional costs which could be incurred in appealing to the Commissioners (and possibly going to the High Court and beyond) mean that most firms reluctantly accept the Revenue view.

Debtors and valuation of work in progress

A firm's accounts ought to take in unpaid fees rendered before the year end — unless the firm is on the **cash basis**.

Work in progress ought also to be brought into account at the lower of cost or realisable value. Many firms have a standard approach to valuing work in progress such as 50 per cent of time costs. However, in strictness partner time ought to be excluded altogether since this is not a cost to the firm, but in effect part of its profit.

Such profit ought not to be anticipated. In some cases the firm's accounts may include partner time in valuing work in progress, but a special adjustment is made when producing tax computations in order to take this amount out of profits for Schedule D Case II purposes.

Partners' salaries and/or interest

Many partnership agreements provide for partners to receive a notional salary or interest on their capital in the firm.

These are proper commercial adjustments and there is some logic in partners receiving a basic salary etc as a first charge before arriving at profits which are then divided according to the partners' respective interests in the firm.

However, for tax purposes a partner's salary or interest are regarded as merely a way of arriving at his or her share of profits. Thus, they are items which are 'added back' in order to arrive at the firm's taxable profits.

EXAMPLE

Tony, Derek and Frances are in partnership. Each partner receives a salary of £30,000 and interest on partnership capital (contributed 40 per cent each by Tony and Derek and 20 per cent by Frances). Suppose the figures are as follows:

	£
Net profits	200,000
Less Partners' salaries	90,000
	110,000
Less Partners' interest (say)	50,000
Net profit per accounts	60,000

The division of the profits for tax purposes might then be:

	Tony (40%) £	Derek (40%) £	Frances (20%) £	Total £
Net profits	24,000	24,000	12,000	60,000
Add back partners' salaries	30,000	30,000	30,000	90,000
partners' interest	20,000	20,000	10,000	50,000
Profits assessable under Schedule D Case II	74,000	74,000	52,000	200,000

Preceding year basis of assessment

If your firm is on the **PY basis**, this can result in a mis-match between your profits for a year and the taxable profits. Thus, if you were a **salaried partner** taxed under Schedule E during your firm's year ended 31 March 1994, and you then became an **'equity partner'**, you will be taxed for 1994/95 on a share of the firm's profits for the year ended 31 March 1994.

EXAMPLE

Dorothy was a salaried partner until 31 March 1994 when she became an equity partner entitled to 30 per cent of the firm's profits. The firm's accounts for the year ended 31 March 1994 show taxable profits of £180,000 (after deducting Dorothy's salary of £45,000).

If the partners make a **continuation election** Dorothy's taxable income for 1994/95 will be 30 per cent of £180,000 ie £54,000.

In effect, Dorothy's Schedule D profits are reduced by a share of the salary paid to her when she was a salaried partner. On the other hand, if there were a lot of disallowable expenses during the year ended 31 March 1994 Dorothy would also be taxed on 30 per cent of these.

This is, of course, one complication which will fall away once the CY basis of assessment comes into operation.

Interest payments and annuities to former partners

Another confusing aspect is that certain expenses borne by an individual partner are not allowable in computing the firm's profits but are allowable as a deduction from the partner's income. Examples of this are interest paid to banks and other UK lenders on loans used to finance partnership capital or the provision of loans to the firm, and annuity payments to former partners.

Interest

Where interest is paid on borrowings taken by the firm, the interest is simply an expense in arriving at the firm's profits. On the other hand, where a partner has borrowed personally, the interest is a charge against his income. To qualify for relief in this way, the following conditions need to be satisfied:

(1) There must be a fixed loan rather than an overdraft;
(2) The loan must be applied as the payment into the firm of partnership capital or as a loan by the partner to the firm;
(3) The borrower must not have withdrawn the capital/loan from the firm (if he has done so, a corresponding part of the loan interest ceases to be eligible for tax relief).

Until 1993/94, there was a further condition: that the lender must be a UK bank, or a UK branch of a foreign bank or a person who is subject to tax on the interest under Schedule D Case III. This condition no longer applies because of FA 1994, s 81.

Interest which falls due for payment in a year is allowed as a deduction from the partner's general income provided it has been paid. If the interest is actually paid in a later tax year, it is then treated as an allowable deduction against the partner's income for the year that it is paid.

Because the interest is a charge against the partner's general income, it can be deducted from any of his income, ie not just from his partnership income.

In many cases, the firm arrange a loan for an incoming partner and the firm may also deal with the payment of interest on his behalf, with the interest being charged to his current account. Nevertheless, the loan is a personal loan and must be treated in the way described above.

Annuities to former partners

Where a payment is made to a former proprietor of the practice or a former partner, relief is due if the annuity is an annual payment arising from a liability incurred for full consideration in connection with the acquisition of the practice or an interest in the firm.

The procedure here is that the annuity should be paid net of tax at the basic rate. The annuitant can recover some or all of this tax if he is not liable for the full amount withheld. The partner who pays the annuity can deduct the 'grossed up' amount when computing his liability for higher rate tax.

EXAMPLE

Stewart agreed to retire from the firm if the four remaining partners agreed to pay him an annuity of £10,000 per annum. The annuity is paid 'net of tax' so that Stewart actually receives £7,500.

The £10,000 may be deducted in the firm's accounts but it is not an allowable deduction for tax purposes and it should therefore be 'added back'. However, the partners are entitled to higher rate relief on their share of the £10,000 payment.

Interest and annuities allowed on an 'actual' basis

Even where the firm's profits are assessed on the preceding year basis, the amount allowed against a partner's income for charges is determined by what is actually paid during the tax year.

Capital allowances

Allowances are due to a firm of solicitors in respect of expenditure on plant and machinery. Allowances may also be due on the cost of commercial premises situated in an Enterprise Zone.

A firm must notify relevant expenditure to the Revenue within two years of the tax year concerned, ie eligible expenditure during a firm's year ended 31 January 1995 will normally need to be notified to the Revenue by 5 April 1998, ie profits assessable 1995/96 (PY basis), so the deadline is two years from 5 April 1996. Obviously there may be tighter deadlines in future under the CY basis, especially for a firm with a 31 March year end.

What is plant and machinery?

Until the Finance Act 1994 was enacted, there was no definition of 'plant and machinery' within the Taxes Acts. Even now the position remains unclear. The statutory definition focuses mainly on items which are not considered to be plant because they form part of a building. The Revenue's practice and interpretation is therefore still largely based on decisions handed down by the Courts.

The earliest judicial definition was provided in *Yarmouth v France* (1887) 19 QBD 647, in which Lindley LJ stated:

> ... in its ordinary sense, it includes whatever apparatus is used by a businessman for carrying on his business — not his stock-in-trade, which he buys or makes for sale, but all goods or chattels, fixed or movable, live or dead, which he keeps for permanent employment in his business ...

Some items are obviously within this definition, eg typewriters, dictating machines, telephone equipment, computers, manufacturing equipment, vans and other motor vehicles. What is less obvious is that a building may contain items which are plant and machinery. In some cases the plant will have become part of the building, eg a lift. Capital allowances are also due on building work which is needed to enable plant and machinery to be installed — this would apply if a floor had to be strengthened in order to install a safe or a computer.

The following items of expenditure which may be incurred by a firm of solicitors are normally accepted by the Inland Revenue as constituting plant even though many of them relate to items which effectively become part of a building:

Aerials
Air conditioning
Alarms
Blinds
Boilers
Car Park lighting
Catering equipment and fittings
Cleaning cradles
Clocks
Computer room modification
Computers, fax and telephone equipment
Counters, cabinets and fittings
Curtains

Data transmission equipment
Demountable partitioning
Desks and chairs
Display lighting
Doormats
Dust extraction equipment
Electrical wiring closely related to items of plant such as word
   processors, computers, etc
Fans
Fire alarms
Fire extinguishers
Floodlighting
Gas installations after main connection
Hand driers
Heating and ventilation installation
Hot water pipes
Letter boxes
Lifts
Mirrors
Moveable advertising boards and screens
Moveable screens for display
Public address and intercom systems
Radiators
Reinforced flooring for plant
Removable racking and cupboards
Safes and strong room doors
Sanitary ware
Security cameras
Showers, WCs and wash basins
Shutters
Signs
Sprinkler systems
Staff lockers
Suspended flooring for computer cabling
Telephone equipment
Towel rails and dispensers
Vacuum cleaning equipment
Waste disposal systems
Water heaters
Water softening plant
Window cleaning equipment

Any expenditure on the building which is incurred in connection with the installation of plant and machinery also qualifies for capital allowances as if it were expenditure on plant (CAA 1990, s 66).

How capital allowances are computed

We no longer have first year allowances, instead relief is given by a system of 'writing-down allowances'.

Writing-down allowances are computed on the balance of the 'pool' at the year end. The opening balance of the pool represents the cost of plant and machinery brought forward from previous years, less the capital allowances already received. A firm receives writing-down allowances based on the opening balance plus the cost of additional plant and machinery acquired during the year less any disposal proceeds.

EXAMPLE

Luke and Jean are in partnership. In their year to 31 March 1994 they had purchased plant and machinery at a cost of £30,000 and received capital allowances of £7,500.

During their year ended 31 March 1995, they sell some of this plant for £2,000 and buy new plant for £20,000. Their pool would be as follows:

	£
Written-down value brought forward at 1 April 1994	22,500
Additions during year ended 31 March 1995	20,000
	42,500
Less disposal proceeds	2,000
	40,500
Writing-down allowances (25 per cent)	10,125
Written-down value carried forward	30,375

Assets which are kept separate from the pool

Motor cars which cost more than £12,000 (£8,000 prior to 11 March 1992) need to be kept separate. The maximum writing-down allowance for such a car is £3,000, but a balancing allowance (or charge) arises on disposal.

EXAMPLE

Coke & Co make up accounts to 30 April. On 1 May 1992 the firm acquired a car which cost £30,000 and this is used by an employee. After two years, the car is sold for £10,000.

The car is deemed to be in a separate pool and the position is as follows:

		£
Year 1	Cost	30,000
	writing-down allowance	3,000
		27,000
Year 2	writing-down allowance	3,000
		24,000
Year 3	disposal proceeds	10,000
	Balancing allowance	14,000

Assets used privately by partners must also be kept in a separate pool, eg partners' cars. If a partner has 30 per cent private use, the firm is entitled to only 70 per cent of the writing-down allowance. Thus, if the above car had been used by a partner the annual writing-down allowance would be reduced to £2,100 (£3,000 × 70%) and the balancing allowance would be £9,800 (£14,000 × 70%).

Capital allowances basis period

Where a firm is assessed on the PY basis, the basis period for capital allowances is normally the same period. Thus, if your firm makes up accounts to 30 June, and you are assessed on the PY basis for 1995/96, capital allowances will also be calculated by reference to the year ended 30 June 1994.

Where a firm is assessed on the CY basis, capital allowances are treated as an expense and deducted from profits for the year.

Adjustments between current accounts

Some firms have arrangements whereby adjustments are made between partners' current accounts. Thus, your partnership agreement may provide that the cost of insuring partners lives shall be borne evenly by the partners even though the insurance company charges a higher premium for older partners or those with health problems.

Another situation in which an expense may be charged to a partner's current account is where bad debts are charged to the partner responsible for the client and some care is necessary to ensure that relief is obtained for any expenditure which is tax deductible.

We cover this type of adjustment in more detail in Chapter 13.

Chapter 7

Capital gains tax in relation to the firm

In this chapter, we look at the basic ground rules which determine the way in which capital gains are computed.

We then examine various aspects of capital gains tax which may be relevant to solicitors — whether you are a sole practitioner or partner in a professional firm.

GENERAL

- Background.
- How capital gains are calculated.
- Assets held at 31 March 1982.
- Transitional relief.
- Indexation.

SOLE PRACTITIONERS

- Disposals of business assets.
- Roll-over relief.
- Other reliefs.

PARTNERSHIPS

- Special rules for disposals of partnership assets.
- Asset revaluations and changes in partners.
- Roll-over relief for partners.
- Other reliefs.

GENERAL

Background

All individuals who are either **resident** or **ordinarily resident** at the date of a disposal of a chargeable asset are within the charge to capital gains tax.

Certain disposals are left out of account, so that no charge arises on a disposal to a spouse, provided the married couple are living together at some point during the tax year. Gifts of chargeable assets to charities are exempt. There are also certain types of exempt assets on which no capital gain or loss is deemed to arise — see Appendix 1.

On the other hand, 'disposal' has a wide meaning and can apply to a sale with payment by instalments, a conditional sale (disposal is deemed to take place at the point in time when the contract becomes unconditional), exercise of an option, exchanges of property, gifts, and a disposal which occurs when a property is compulsorily purchased.

Since the introduction of Independent Taxation in 1990/91, an individual's capital gains are computed separately from those of his or her spouse. Any capital losses for the year are set against capital gains and the individual may then deduct his **annual exemption** (currently £5,800). If there are still capital gains which remain chargeable for the year, a further deduction is made for any allowable losses realised in earlier years and which have not already been utilised. The balance (if any) is then subject to capital gains tax. The rate of tax is normally determined as if the chargeable gains were added to the individual's income and charged as if they were income. Thus, the rate of tax can be 40 per cent.

Capital gains tax falls due for payment on 1 December following the end of the tax year in which the capital gain arises.

How capital gains are calculated

We are not going to cover all aspects of computing capital gains in this chapter, but we are going to concentrate on the rules which apply to assets likely to be sold by solicitors because they are in practice. We would recommend that you use a standard reference book such as the *Allied Dunbar Tax Handbook* if you wish to ascertain the way in which capital gains will be computed on disposals of assets owned by you in your private capacity such as shares, property etc.

Sale proceeds

The general rule is that an individual is required to bring into account the full amount of consideration receivable by him, whether or not some of that consideration is payable by instalments. Moreover, the legislation requires market value to be substituted for the actual sale proceeds if the bargain is not at arms-length or is a disposal to a connected person such as a relative. Bear in mind that the Taxation of Chargeable Gains Act 1992 defines 'connected person' so as to include a partner and this could therefore have a bearing on the position if you should dispose of an asset used in your practice to one of your partners.

It is possible that you may dispose of an asset on terms such that part of the proceeds may be returned if certain contingent liabilities arise. In such a situation, the legislation requires the capital gain to be charged initially on the full sale proceeds. If, in fact, the contingent liability becomes an actual liability and the vendor is required to refund part of the sale proceeds, his capital gains tax assessment is adjusted to reflect the reduced sale consideration.

Bear in mind that a disposal is normally regarded as taking place at the time that an unconditional contract is entered into, even though completion and payment may follow later. Where a conditional contract is made, the disposal is deemed to take place at the point in time when the condition is satisfied and the conditional contract becomes unconditional.

What costs are allowable?

The legislation permits only a limited range of expenses to be deducted in computing capital gains and losses. Section 38 of the TCGA 1992 states:

(1)   Except as otherwise expressly provided, the sums allowable as a deduction from the consideration in the computation of the gain accruing to a person on the disposal of an asset shall be restricted to:

   a)   the amount or value of the consideration, in money or money's worth, given by him or on his behalf wholly and exclusively for the acquisition of the asset, together with the incidental costs to him of the acquisition or, if the asset was not acquired by him, any expenditure wholly and exclusively incurred by him in providing the asset;

b)   the amount of any expenditure wholly and exclusively
      incurred on the asset by him or on his behalf for the
      purpose of enhancing the value of the asset, being
      expenditure reflected in the state or nature of the asset
      at the time of the disposal, and any expenditure wholly
      and exclusively incurred by him in establishing, preserving
      or defending his title to, or to a right over, the asset;
c)   the incidental costs to him of making the disposal.

Acquisition cost

It follows from the above definition that a deduction may be taken
for the acquisition cost of the asset. In fact, the legislation extends
this so that the market value of the asset at 31 March 1982 may
be taken instead of the cost — provided the vendor held the asset
at that date (see below on rebasing). In certain special circumstances
it may even be possible to deduct the asset's market value at 6
April 1965.

Incidental costs of the acquisition

These are restricted to the following:

- Fees, commission or remuneration paid to a surveyor, valuer,
  auctioneer, accountant, agent or legal advisor;
- Transfer/conveyancing charges (including stamp duty); and
- Advertising to find a seller.

Enhancement expenditure

The legislation permits a deduction to be claimed in respect of
expenditure which has been incurred in order to enhance the value
of the asset provided that such expenditure is reflected in the state
or nature of the asset at the time of disposal. The latter condition
excludes relief for improvements which have worn out by the time
that the asset is disposed of.

Incidental costs of disposal

The following expenses may be deducted under this head:

- Fees, commission or remuneration for the professional
  services of a surveyor, valuer, auctioneer, accountant, agent
  or legal advisor;

- Transfer, conveyancing charges in connection with the sale;
- Advertising to find a buyer;
- Any other costs reasonably incurred in making any valuation or apportionment for capital gains tax purposes, including expenses reasonably incurred in ascertaining the asset's market value where this is required. The Revenue draw a distinction between the costs of making a valuation and fees incurred in negotiating with the Revenue and take the view that the latter costs are not allowable.

Assets held at 31 March 1982 — 'rebasing'

Where an asset was held at 31 March 1982, the capital gain may be computed as if the value at 31 March 1982 were the cost. Technically, the legislation requires a statutory hypothesis that the asset was sold and immediately reacquired at its market value at that time. This is known as 'rebasing'.

It is possible that the original cost of the asset may still be relevant if:

1) A loss arises when using the March 1982 value and a smaller loss arises if the loss is computed by reference to original cost. Only the smaller loss is allowable.
2) A gain arises using the March 1982 value, but a smaller gain arises by reference to the original cost (ie situations where original cost was more than the market value of the asset at 31 March 1982). Only the smaller gain is assessable.
3) Where a gain arises when one has regard to original cost, but a loss arises when one takes the 31 March 1982 value (or the other way round), the position is regarded as producing neither a chargeable gain nor an allowable loss for capital gains tax purposes.

However, if a universal rebasing election has been made the above restrictions do not apply and any capital gain or loss is calculated solely by reference to the 31 March 1982 value.

Universal rebasing election

The legislation permits an individual to elect for the rebasing rule to be applied to all disposals of assets held by him at 31 March 1982. In such a situation, the original cost is completely ignored, and gains/losses are calculated only by reference to the 31 March 1982 value.

A universal rebasing election is irrevocable and applies to all assets held at 31 March 1982.

The legislation requires a universal rebasing election to be made within two years of the end of the tax year in which a disposal first takes place of assets which were held both at 6 April 1988 and at 31 March 1982. If you have not made an election and you made any disposals during the period 6 April 1988 — 5 April 1992 of assets held at 31 March 1982, it is now too late to make the election.

An election may be made by each spouse. However, where assets pass from one spouse to the other, and the recipient subsequently disposes of the asset, the gain or loss on that particular asset is determined by whether the transferor spouse had made the universal rebasing election.

Market value at 6 April 1965

There can be exceptional circumstances where it is necessary to ascertain the market value of an asset at 6 April 1965, where the vendor owned the asset prior to that date. However, this complication can arise only where the value at 6 April 1965 was higher than the 31 March 1982 value — which is relatively rare.

Transitional relief

Rebasing was introduced in 1988/89. Prior to that, an individual's gains were computed by reference to actual cost and not by reference to the asset's value at 31 March 1982. Transitional relief is available where the following conditions are satisfied:

- You have received a gift of an asset between 1 April 1982 and 5 April 1988;
- The donor's gain was **held-over**; and
- The donor held the asset at 31 March 1982.

The relief may also be available if you have claimed roll-over relief in respect of an asset held at 31 March 1982 and which was sold between 1 April 1982 and 5 April 1988.

The relief takes the form of an increase in your acquisition value by means of a special adjustment equal to half of the held-over or rolled-over gain.

Basically, the adjustment made is that the acquisition value is deemed to be increased by half of the gain which has been held-over or rolled-over.

EXAMPLE

Dorothy owned half of the goodwill of a firm at 31 March 1982. In June 1987, she sold this and realised a gain of £130,000.

In May 1988, she re-invested the sale proceeds in the acquisition of another practice (see below re **Roll-over relief**).

The transitional relief means that her cost of the new practice is reduced by only half of the rolled-over gain of £130,000.

Indexation

Capital gains tax is charged on real capital gains. An individual who makes a capital gain is therefore allowed to increase his acquisition value by an amount reflecting the increase in the retail price index (RPI) between March 1982 (or the date of acquisition if later) and the month in which the asset is disposed of. The following formula must be used:

$$\frac{RD - RI}{RI}$$

Where RD = the RPI figure for the month of disposal and RI = the RPI figure for the month of investment or acquisition.

EXAMPLE

In January 1994, Karen disposes of a property used in her practice for £213,000. It cost £78,000 in January 1983 and Karen extended it in January 1990 at a cost of £22,000. Karen is due indexation allowance on £78,000 for the period January 1983 to January 1994 and on £22,000 for the period January 1990 to January 1994.

Karen's capital gain is:

		£
Sale Proceeds		213,000
Less cost		100,000
Gain before indexation		113,000
Indexation on 1983 cost	32,214	
Indexation on 1990 expenditure	4,013	36,227
		76,773

Following the Finance Act 1994, indexation relief may only reduce or extinguish a capital gain, it cannot convert a gain into a loss or increase a loss. A different rule applied up to 30 November 1993 in that indexation relief could create an allowable loss. Transitional measures may permit an individual to have the benefit of up to £10,000 indexation losses on transactions entered into between 30 November 1993 and 5 April 1995.

SOLE PRACTITIONERS

Disposals of business assets

A sole practitioner may realise a capital gain on the disposal of his office premises, or he may dispose of goodwill on selling his practice or admitting a partner.

Roll-over relief

Roll-over relief may be available where a person sells an asset which is used by him in his practice and re-invests in qualifying replacement assets used for business purposes.

A gain is said to be 'rolled over' because it is not charged to tax, but is deducted from the acquisition cost of the new assets.

EXAMPLE

Alan sells the office block from which his firm practices and realises £190,000. His capital gain is £100,000. He then re-invests £200,000 in the acquisition of premises for a new practice.

By claiming roll-over relief, Alan avoids having to pay tax on the gain of £100,000. The acquisition cost of the new assets is reduced as follows:

	£
Actual cost	200,000
Less rolled-over gain	100,000
Deemed acquisition cost	100,000

The relief is really a form of deferment since a larger gain will normally arise on a subsequent disposal of the replacement asset.

Conditions which need to be satisfied

The asset that has been disposed of must have been used in a practice (or other business) and must have fallen into one of the following categories:

- Land and buildings.
- Fixed plant and machinery.
- Goodwill.
- Assets which do not apply to a firm of solicitors, ie ships, various farming quotas, aircraft, hovercraft, satellites and spacecraft.

The replacement assets must also fall into one of these categories, but not necessarily the same category as the original asset. Moreover, the replacement assets can be used in a different trade or profession.

The replacement assets must normally be acquired within a period starting one year before the date of the disposal of the original asset and ending three years after the date of disposal. The time limit can be extended (at the Revenue's discretion) if the acquisition of replacement assets within three years was not possible because of circumstances outside the person's control.

Restriction on relief where not all the sale proceeds are re-invested

Roll-over relief is dependent on the individual re-investing at least part of his capital gain. Relief is restricted if only part of the sale proceeds are re-invested.

EXAMPLE

Suppose Alan had re-invested only £140,000, the roll-over relief would be reduced by the amount of the sale proceeds not re-invested ie £50,000 (£190,000 – £140,000).

The £50,000 capital gain which is not covered by roll-over relief will then be subject to tax in the normal way.

Roll-over relief where replacement assets are wasting assets

Special rules apply where the replacement expenditure consists of the purchase of a wasting asset (ie an asset with an expected useful life of less than 50 years) or an asset which will become a wasting asset within ten years. The capital gain in these circumstances is not deferred indefinitely, but becomes chargeable on the first of the following occasions:

- The disposal of the replacement asset; or
- The asset ceasing to be used in the business; or
- The expiry of ten years.

Plant and machinery is always considered to have a useful life of less than 50 years. Furthermore, the acquisition of a lease with less than 60 years to run will also constitute the acquisition of a wasting asset. However, the goodwill of a business is not regarded as a wasting asset.

EXAMPLE

1) Brian sells his practice and re-invests in a 59 year lease of office premises which he uses in his new practice. In the sixth year the offices are let out as an investment.

   The rolled-over gain would become chargeable in year 6.

2) Christopher also rolls over into a 59 year lease. He is still using the property after ten years, but because it has become a wasting asset within that period, the rolled-over gain becomes chargeable in year ten.

Reinvestment in non-wasting assets

A capital gain which has been rolled over into the purchase of the wasting assets can be transferred if the person acquires new non-wasting replacement assets during the ten-year period. Thus, if in example 1 above Brian had bought the goodwill of a business in year five he could transfer his roll-over relief claim to the new asset. No gain would then become chargeable in year six when he lets the office premises.

Other reliefs

There are two reliefs worth mentioning here: retirement relief and re-investment relief for gains which are re-invested in qualifying unquoted companies.

Retirement relief

This is a special relief for gains realised on the disposal of a business by an individual aged 55 or over, we cover this in detail in Chapter 15.

Re-investment relief

This is a new relief which was introduced in the Finance Act 1993 and greatly extended by the Finance Act 1994. It permits any gain realised after 29 November 1993 by an individual (or trustee) to be deferred where the gain is re-invested in one or more qualifying unquoted trading companies.

Re-investment must take the form of ordinary shares. Moreover, the re-investment must be made during a period from one year before the gain until three years after the gain was realised.

The company is a qualifying company only if it carries on a trade and does not carry on various 'prohibited' activities, ie:

1) Dealing in land, in commodities of futures or in shares, securities or other financial instruments;
2) Dealing in goods otherwise than in the course of any ordinary trade of wholesale or retail distribution;
3) Banking, insurance, money-lending, debt factoring, hire-purchase financing or other financial activities;
4) Oil extraction activities;
5) Leasing (including letting ships on charter or other assets on hire) or receiving royalties or licence fees;
6) Providing legal or accountancy services;
7) Providing services or facilities for any trade carried on by another person (other than a parent company) which consists to any substantial extent of activities within any of the paragraphs above and in which a controlling interest is held by a person who also has a controlling interest in the trade carried on by the company;
8) Property development;
9) Farming.

The relief is clawed back where a company ceases to meet the qualifying conditions within three years of the re-investment. The gain is treated as arising at the point in time when the conditions are breached.

A claw-back may also arise where the individual who has qualified for re-investment relief ceases to be resident in the United Kingdom within the three year period.

PARTNERSHIPS

A partnership is not a taxable entity for capital gains tax purposes.

Where a partnership asset is sold at a capital gain (or loss), the gain is divided amongst the partners in accordance with their profit-sharing ratios. Each partner is personally assessable on his share of the gain.

The partner's actual capital gains tax liability will depend upon his own situation, ie whether he has other gains for the year, has available losses, can claim roll-over relief or is entitled to retirement relief.

Special rules for disposals of partnership assets

Nevertheless, the position can be complicated and there are a number of special rules for partners. The Inland Revenue set out their practice in 1975 — see Appendix 2 to this chapter.

Partnership's acquisition value

Although individual partners' entitlement to profits may vary over the years, the partnership's acquisition value for the firm's chargeable assets is not affected unless there are cash payments from one partner to another to acquire a greater interest in the firm or unless assets are revalued as part of the arrangements for changes in profit-sharing.

Assets held by the firm at 31 March 1982

The partnership may make a universal rebasing election for partnership assets owned at 31 March 1982. Their market value at that date will then be used instead of cost. This election may be made independently of the individual partners' position in relation to their personal assets when a disposal of such an asset takes place. Moreover, there may be partners who were not in the partnership at 31 March 1982, but this does not affect the computation of the gain.

Asset revaluations and changes in partners

The tax implications need to be watched very carefully where a partnership has substantial assets which are worth more than their 'book value' (ie the value at which they are shown in the firm's accounts) and there is a change in partners or in their profit sharing ratios.

A revaluation to bring the book value of the assets into line with their market value can produce a liability for individual partners if there is a reduction in their profit-sharing ratios, as commonly happens when new partners are introduced.

EXAMPLE

Andrew is a partner in a five partner firm and is entitled to 20 per cent of the profits. He retires and his colleagues then share profits on the basis of 25 per cent each.

As part of the arrangements for his retirement, the book value of the firm's office block is increased from £150,000 to its current market value of £750,000. The surplus is credited to each partner's account so that Andrew is credited with £120,000.

Andrew is treated as if he had realised a gain on the disposal of a one-fifth share of the building. This would be based on the £120,000.

The remaining four partners are not treated as having made a disposal. Indeed, they each have made an acquisition of a five-per-cent interest in the building for an outlay of £30,000.

Much the same would apply if Andrew continued as a partner but accepted a much lower profit share for the future.

EXAMPLE

Bruce and Charles are partners. Their lease on the office premises is not included in their firm's balance sheet because no capital payment was involved but the lease is now worth £90,000. Bruce and Charles agree to admit David as an equal partner in return for his paying in new capital into the firm of £75,000. They revalue the premises before admitting David as a partner, and the surplus of £90,000 is credited to their accounts.

In this case, Bruce and Charles will each be regarded as having made a disposal of a one-sixth interest in the premises. This is because David's new capital will go into the firm as a whole. After coming in, he effectively owns one-third of all the assets (and is responsible for one-third of the liabilities).

The former partners' interest in the premises has been reduced from 50 per cent to a one-third interest.

Partnership changes without revaluation

The position is quite different where partners join or leave and there is no revaluation of assets. In such a case, the remaining or incoming partners normally take over the outgoing partners' acquisition values for the firm's assets.

EXAMPLE

Anthony and Ben are in partnership. They own premises which have a book value of £90,000 (equal to cost in 1983). Anthony retires and is replaced by Carl. The premises are not revalued but are actually worth £200,000.

Later the premises are sold for £240,000. Ben and Carl are assessed on their share of the gain.

The gain will be computed by reference to the firm's original cost of £90,000, not the premises' market value at the time that Carl became a partner.

This treatment does not apply where the partners are connected persons (perhaps because they are relatives), or where cash payments are made to acquire an interest in the firm. In such a case, a capital gain may arise based on the market value of the firm's chargeable assets.

EXAMPLE

In the above example, suppose Carl had bought Anthony's interest in the firm for £175,000. Carl's capital gain on the sale of the premises would reflect the part of the £175,000 referable to the premises. His position might well be as follows:

	£
Share of disposal proceeds	120,000
Less market value at date of admission to the firm	100,000
Capital gain	20,000
Ben's capital gain is likely to be: Share of disposal proceeds	120,000
Less share of original cost	45,000
Capital gain	75,000

Roll-over relief for partners

Roll-over relief for partnerships works in a similar way to sole practitioners (see p 91). However, there are three additional aspects to be borne in mind for partners.

Roll-over claims are an individual decision

Each partner is treated separately. He can either roll-over his capital gain or choose not to do so. If a partner leaves and sets up his own practice, he may be entitled to roll-over relief whereas his former partners may not incur any expenditure on qualifying replacement assets.

Purchase of assets by one partner from another

A partner who acquires a larger share of goodwill by buying another partner's interest may secure roll-over relief for this expenditure.

Assets owned by one particular partner

Where one partner owns property used by the firm (eg the firm's office premises), he may be entitled to claim roll-over on a sale — provided of course that he re-invests in qualifying assets. There is no restriction on roll-over relief where the partner has charged rent.

Other reliefs

Retirement relief and re-investment relief must also be borne in mind. We cover these on p 188 and p 94 respectively.

Appendix 1 — exempt assets for capital gains tax

No gain is treated as arising on the disposal of any of the following:

foreign currency acquired for personal expenditure;
decoration awarded for valour or gallant conduct;
rights under a life assurance policy, unless acquired for money;
an interest under a settlement, unless acquired for money;
debts;
covenants;
chattels which are wasting assets[1];
chattels disposed of for less than £6,000;
principal private residence;
government stock;
qualifying corporate bonds;
works of art;
shares acquired under Business Expansion Scheme from which relief has not been withdrawn;
shares acquired under Enterprise Investment Scheme from which relief has not been withdrawn.

[1] unless the disponor was entitled to claim capital allowances

Appendix 2 — capital gains tax: partnerships

Following discussions with the Law Society and the Allied
Accountancy Bodies the Board of Inland Revenue issued the following
statement of practice on the capital gains tax treatment of partnerships
in 1975.

Capital gains tax: partnerships

The Board of Inland Revenue have had discussions with the Law
Society and the Allied Accountancy Bodies on the capital gains tax
treatment of partnerships. This statement sets out a number of points
of general practice which have been agreed.

1. Nature of the asset liable to tax

[Section 59 of the TCGA 1992] treats any partnership dealings in
chargeable assets for capital gains tax purposes as dealings by the
individual partners rather than by the firm as such. Each partner
has therefore to be regarded as owning a fractional share of each
of the partnership assets and not for this purpose an interest in the
partnership.

Where it is necessary to ascertain the market value of a partner's
share in a partnership asset for capital gains tax purposes, it will
be taken as a fraction of the value of the total partnership interest
in the asset without any discount for the size of his share. If, for
example, a partnership owned all the issued shares in a company,
the value of the interest in that holding of a partner with a one-
tenth share would be one tenth of the value of the partnership's
100 per cent holding.

2. Disposals of assets by a partnership

Where an asset is disposed of by a partnership to an outside party
each of the partners will be treated as disposing of his fractional
share of the asset. Similarly, if a partnership makes a part disposal
of an asset each partner will be treated as making a part disposal
of his fractional share. In computing gains or losses the proceeds
of disposal will be allocated between the partners in the ratio of
their shares in asset surpluses at the time of the disposal. Where
this is not specifically laid down the allocation will follow the actual
destination of the surplus as shown in the partnership accounts; regard
will of course have to be paid to any agreement outside the accounts.

If the surplus is not allocated among the partners but, for example, put to a common reserve regard will be had to the ordinary profit-sharing ratio in the absence of a specified asset surplus sharing ratio. Expenditure on the acquisition of assets by a partnership will be allocated between the partners in the same way at the time of the acquisition. This allocation may require adjustment, however, if there is a subsequent change in the partnership ratios (see paragraph 4).

3.   Partnership assets divided in kind among the partners

Where a partnership distributes an asset in kind to one or more of the partners, for example on dissolution, a partner who receives the asset will not be regarded as disposing of his fractional share in it. A computation will first be necessary of the gains which would be chargeable on the individual partners if the asset had been disposed of at its current market value. Where this results in a gain being attributed to a partner not receiving the asset the gain will be charged at the time of the distribution of the asset. Where, however, the gain is allocated to a partner receiving the asset concerned there will be no charge on distribution. Instead, his capital gains tax cost to be carried forward will be the market value of the asset at the date of distribution as reduced by the amount of his gain. The same principles will be applied where the computation results in a loss.

4.   Changes in partnership sharing ratios (see also Appendix 3 – SP1/89)

An occasion of charge also arises when there is a change in partnership sharing ratios including changes arising from a partner joining or leaving the partnership. In these circumstances a partner who reduces or gives up his share in asset surpluses will be treated as disposing of part of the whole of his share in each of the partnership assets and a partner who increases his share will be treated as making a similar acquisition. Subject to the qualifications mentioned at 6 and 7 below the disposal consideration will be a fraction (equal to the fractional share changing hands) of the current balance sheet value of each chargeable asset provided that there is no direct payment of consideration outside the partnership. Where no adjustment is made through the partnership accounts (for example, by revaluation of the assets coupled with a corresponding increase or decease in partner's current or capital account at some date between the partner's acquisition and the reduction in his share) the disposal is treated as made for a consideration equal to his capital gains tax cost and thus there will be neither a chargeable gain nor an allowable loss at that point. A partner whose share reduces will carry forward a smaller proportion of cost to set against a subsequent disposal of the asset and a partner whose share increases will carry forward a larger proportion of cost.

The general rules in [TCGA 1992, s 42] for apportioning the total acquisition cost on a part disposal of an asset will not be applied in the case of partner reducing his asset surplus share. Instead, the cost of the part disposed of will be calculated on a fractional basis.

5. Adjustments through the accounts

Where a partnership asset is revalued a partner will be credited in his current or capital account with a sum equal to his fractional share of the increase in value. An upward revaluation of chargeable assets is not itself an occasion of charge. If, however, there were to be a subsequent reduction in the partner's asset surplus share, the effect would be to reduce his potential liability to capital gains tax on the eventual disposal of the assets without an equivalent reduction of the credit he has received in the accounts. Consequently at the time of the reduction in sharing ratio he will be regarded as disposing of the fractional share of the partnership asset represented by the difference between his old and his new share for a consideration equal to that fraction of the increased value at the revaluation. The partner whose share correspondingly increases will have his acquisition cost to be carried forward for the asset increased by the same amount. The same principles will be applied in the case of a downward revaluation.

6. Payments outside the accounts

Where on a change of partnership sharing ratios payments are made directly between two or more partners outside the framework of the partnership accounts, the payments represent consideration for the disposal of the whole or part of a partner's share in partnership assets in addition to any consideration calculated on the bases described in 4 and 5 above. Often such payments will be for goodwill not included in the balance sheet. In such cases the partner receiving the payment will have no capital gains tax cost to set against it unless he made a similar payment for his share in the asset (for example, on entering the partnership) or elects to have the market value at 6 April 1965 treated as his acquisition cost. The partner making the payment will only be allowed to deduct the amount

in computing gains or losses on a subsequent disposal of his share
in the asset. He will be able to claim a loss when he finally leaves
the partnership or when his share is reduced provided that he then
receives either no consideration or a lesser consideration for his share
of the asset. Where the payment clearly constitutes payment for a
share in assets included in the partnership accounts, the partner
receiving it will be able to deduct the amount of the partnership
acquisition cost represented by the fraction he is disposing of. Special
treatment, as outlined in 7 below, may be necessary for transfers
between persons not at arm's length.

7.   *Transfers between persons at arm's length*

Where no payment is made either through or outside the accounts
in connection with a change in partnership sharing ratio, a capital
gains tax charge will only arise if the transaction is otherwise than
by way of a bargain made at arm's length and falls therefore within
[TCGA 1992, s 18(2)] for transactions between connected persons.
Under [TCGA 1992, s 286(4)] transfers of partnership assets between
partners are not regarded as transactions between connected persons
if they are pursuant to bona fide commercial arrangements. This
treatment will also be given to transactions between an incoming
partner and the existing partners.

Where the partners (including incoming partners) are connected
other than by partnership (for example, father and son) or are
otherwise not at arm's length (for example, uncle and nephew) the
transfer of a share in the partnership assets may fall to be treated
as having been made at market value. Market value will not be
substituted, however, if nothing would have been paid had the parties
been at arm's length. Similarly if consideration of less than market
value passes between partners connected other than by partnership
or otherwise not at arm's length, the transfer will only be regarded
as having been made for full market value if the consideration actually
paid was less than that which would have been paid by parties at
arm's length. Where a transfer has to be treated as if it had taken
place for market value, the deemed disposal proceeds will fall to
be treated in the same way as payments outside the accounts.

8.   *Annuities provided by partnerships*

A lump sum which is paid to a partner on leaving the partnership
or on a reduction of his share in the partnership represents
consideration for the disposal by the partner concerned of the whole

or part of his share in the partnership assets and will be subject to the rules in 6 above. The same treatment will apply when a partnership buys a purchased life annuity for a partner, the measure of the consideration being the actual cost of the annuity.

Where a partnership makes annual payments to a retired partner (whether under covenant or not) the capitalised value of the annuity will only be treated as consideration for the disposal of his share in the partnership assets under [TCGA 1992, s 37] if it is more than can be regarded as a reasonable recognition of the past contribution of work and effort by the partner to the partnership. Provided that the former partner had been in the partnership for at least ten years an annuity will be regarded as reasonable for this purpose if it is no more than two-thirds of his average share of the profits in the best three of the last seven years in which he was required to devote substantially the whole of his time to acting as a partner. In arriving at a partner's share of the profits regard will be had to the partnership profits assessed before deduction of any capital allowances or charges. The 10 year period will include any period during which the partner was a member of another firm whose business has been merged with that of the present firm. For lesser periods the following fractions will be used instead of the two-thirds:

Complete years in partnership	Fraction
1–5	$\frac{1}{60}$ for each year
6	$\frac{4}{60}$
7	$\frac{16}{60}$
8	$\frac{24}{60}$
9	$\frac{32}{60}$

Where the capitalised value of an annuity is treated as consideration received by the retired partner, it will also be regarded as allowable expenditure by the remaining partners on the acquisition of their fractional shares in partnership assets from him.

9. Mergers

When the members of two or more existing partnerships come together to form a new one, the capital gains tax treatment will follow the same lines as that for changes in partnership sharing ratios. If gains arise for reasons similar to those covered in 5 and 6 above, it may be possible for roll-over relief under [TCGA 1992, s 152–155] to be claimed by any partner continuing in the partnership in so far as he disposes of part of his share in the assets of the old firm and acquires a share in other assets put into the 'merged' firm. Where, however, in such cases the consideration given for the shares in chargeable assets acquired is less than the consideration for those disposed of, relief will be restricted under [TCGA 1992, s 153].

10.   Shares acquired in stages

Where a share in a partnership is acquired in stages wholly after 5 April 1965, the acquisition costs of the various chargeable assets will be calculated by pooling the expenditure relating to each asset. Where a share built up in stages was acquired wholly or partly before 6 April 1965 the rules in [TCGA 1992, Sched 2] will normally be followed to identify the acquisition cost of the share in each asset which is disposed of on the occasion of a reduction in the partnership's share, ie the disposal will normally be identified with shares acquired on a 'first in, first out' basis. Special consideration will be given, however, to any case in which this rule appears to produce an unreasonable result when applied to temporary changes in the shares in a partnership, for example those occurring when a partner's departure and a new partner's arrival are out of step by a few months.

Appendix 3 — Statement of Practice SP1/89

Rebasing

The Board of Inland Revenue have agreed that a disposal of a share of partnership assets to which paragraph 4 of the Statement of Practice of 17 January 1975 [Appendix 2] applies so that neither a chargeable gain nor an allowable loss accrues (before indexation for disposals before 6 April 1988) may be treated for the purpose of FA 1988, s 96, Sched 8 as if it were a no gain/no loss disposal within FA 1988, Sched 8, para 1 [now TCGA 1992, s 35 and Sched 3].

Deferred charges

A disposal of a share of partnership assets to which paragraph 4 of the Statement of Practice of 17 January 1975 applies so that neither a chargeable gain nor an allowable loss accrues (before indexation for disposals before 6 April 1988) may be treated for the purposes of FA 1988, s 97, Sched 9, as if it were a no gain/no loss disposal within FA 1988, Sched 8, para 1 [TCGA 1992 Sched 3, para 1].

Indexation

When, on or after 6 April 1988, a partner disposes of all or part of his share of partnership assets in circumstances to which paragraph 4 of the *Statement of Practice* of 17 January 1975 applies so that neither a chargeable gain nor an allowable loss accrues, the amount of the consideration will be calculated on the assumption that an unindexed gain will accrue to the transferor equal to the indexation allowance, so that after taking account of the indexation allowance, neither a gain nor a loss accrues.

Where a partner disposes on or after 6 April 1988 of all or part of his share of partnership assets, and he is treated by virtue of this *Statement* as having owned the share on 31 March 1982, the indexation allowance on the disposal may be computed as if he had acquired the share on 31 March 1982. A disposal of a share in a partnership asset on or after 31 March 1982 to which paragraph 4 of the *Statement of Practice* of 17 January 1975 applies so that neither a chargeable gain nor an allowable loss accrues may be treated for the purpose of [TCGA 1992, s 55] as if it were a no gain/no loss disposal within [TCGA 1992, s 55(5)]. A special rule will, however, apply where the share changed hands on or after 6 April 1985

(1 April in the case of an acquisition from a company) and before 6 April 1988: in these circumstances the indexation allowance will be computed by reference to the 31 March 1982 value but from the date of the last disposal of the share before 6 April 1988.

Chapter 8

Miscellaneous tax aspects of a solicitor's practice

In this chapter, we look at some tax aspects of a solicitor's practice which regularly give rise to problems and uncertainty in practice.

- Directors' fees brought into the firm's accounts.
- VAT treatment of insurance commission.
- Interest received on clients' accounts.
- Taxation aspects of the firm's own property transactions.

Director's fees brought into the firm's accounts

A partner in a firm of solicitors may act as a director of a client company. His partners may regard the fees received by the director as a receipt which belongs to the firm rather than personal earnings which belong to the individual in his personal capacity. However, in law the director's fees are chargeable on the individual under Schedule E.

The Inland Revenue have dealt with this by an Extra-statutory Concession A37 which states:

Tax treatment of directors' fees received by partnerships

Where fees are received in respect of directorships held by members of a professional partnership they are in strictness assessable on the individual partners under Schedule E. It is, however, the practice of the Inland Revenue to accede to a request from the partnership for the inclusion of the fees in the Schedule D assessment provided that:

(*a*) the directorship is a normal incident of the profession and of the particular practice concerned;

(*b*)   the fees are only a small part of the profits; and

(*c*)   under the partnership agreement the fees are pooled for division among the partners.

Partnerships seeking such treatment are required to provide the Revenue with a written undertaking that directors' fees received in full will be included in the gross income or receipts of the basis period, whether or not the directorship is still held in the year of assessment and whether or not the partner concerned is still a partner'.

In such a situation the Inland Revenue will normally issue a NT code so that no PAYE is deducted. Moreover, the fees will not normally be subject to a deduction for employee's National Insurance contributions.

The Inland Revenue also operate a similar treatment for sole practitioners who receive director's fees, but the DSS insist on national insurance contributions being paid by the company in the normal way.

VAT treatment of insurance commission

The Law Society has published details of the policy adopted by Customs & Excise on the calculation of VAT when a solicitor's bill is reduced by reason of a rebate of commission to a client (see *Law Society Gazette* 8 March 1989).

VAT has to be calculated on the final (reduced) amount which is charged. Customs & Excise have confirmed that the invoice may be presented in either of two forms:

(i)	Fee normally charged	X
	Rebate equivalent to commission received	Y
		Z
	VAT (17.5% of Z)	V
	Total due	Z+V
or		
(ii)	Fee (net of £Y commission)	Z
	VAT (17.5% of Z)	V
	Total due	Z+V

Where a bill is set out as in (i) above, it is important that the commission amount be described as a rebate. If commission is passed on separately rather than as a reduction of the fee, VAT remains due on the full amount of the fee charged. Another consideration is that commission which is passed on may well attract a tax liability for the recipient.

Interest received on clients' accounts

For many years, the Inland Revenue took the view that where a solicitor did not maintain a separate designated account for a client, interest arising from the deposit was assessable on the solicitor under Schedule D Case III. A payment to the client in lieu of the interest which would have accrued if the money had been deposited in a separate designated account was treated as a deduction for Case II purposes. This had the effect of depressing the solicitor's earnings for Schedule D Case II purposes and had a number of drawbacks (eg it depressed the profits on which the solicitors could base their pension contributions).

However, Inland Revenue *Statement of Practice* A22 now provides that payments in lieu of interest are regarded as the client's income and not the solicitor's income. The solicitor is assessed to income tax only on the net interest retained on undesignated clients' accounts in the year and the interest paid to clients in respect of monies held on such accounts is no longer dealt with as a deduction in computing the profits of the practice.

The Law Society have published a detailed memorandum on the tax treatment of interest earned on various types of client accounts by solicitors and extracts from this are reproduced as Appendix 1 to this chapter.

Taxation aspects of the firm's own property transactions

In this section, we look at some aspects of taking on premises, or disposing of property, which regularly crop up in relation to firms of solicitors.

Rent free periods

The High Court has recently confirmed Customs' interpretation of the VAT implications of rent-free periods. Where a landlord grants a rent-free period which is conditional on certain actions being undertaken by the tenant, such as repairs, refurbishment or modification work to the property, the rent forgone is deemed to be consideration for a supply of services by the tenant and is subject to VAT. However, where there are no such conditions the rent-free period is not deemed to be a VATable supply.

Reverse premiums

A firm of solicitors may be offered a cash inducement payment to take a lease over office premises.

The receipt of such a lump sum payment should not normally affect the firm's right to a Schedule D Case II deduction for the rent. However, if the rent is increased by the landlord to take account of the payment of a reverse premium, there is a risk that the excess rent will not be deductible.

Leading Counsel has in the past advised that a typical reverse premium will not normally constitute an income receipt since:

- it is inherently of a capital nature. It is a 'once and for all' payment and has all the characteristics of a capital rather than a revenue receipt;
- it is not in the nature of a professional or trading receipt in the course of the tenant's trade or profession;
- it is not a payment in return for a service to the landlord within Case VI;
- it is not a subsidy towards a revenue expense (provided, of course, the rent is no more than a proper market rent);
- it is not an adventure in the nature of trade by the tenant;
- it is not normally a contribution towards capital expenditure which falls within Capital Allowances Act 1990, s 153.

Value Added Tax

Where a firm receives a reverse premium it must normally account for VAT at standard rate on the monies received.

Surrender of existing lease in return for new lease

Technically a disposal occurs for capital gains tax purposes where a lease is surrendered in consideration for a new lease being granted. In practice, however, the Inland Revenue has usually ignored such disposals provided that the tenant does not receive a capital sum for the surrender of the old lease and the terms of the new lease are broadly comparable to those of the old lease. An Extra-statutory Concession (D39) provides as follows:

> In practice, the surrender of a lease before its expiry and the grant of a new lease for a longer term will not be regarded as a disposal or part disposal of the old lease where all the following conditions are met:
>
> (i) the transaction is between unconnected parties bargaining at arm's length;
>
> (ii) the transaction is not part of or connected with a larger scheme or series of transactions;
>
> (iii) a capital sum is not received by the lessee;
>
> (iv) the extent of the property in which the lessee has an interest under the new lease does not differ in any way from that to which the old lease related;
>
> (v) the terms of the new lease (other than its duration and the amount of rent payable) do not differ from those of the old lease.

Compensation

A firm may receive compensation on having to vacate premises, either because of a compulsory purchase order or under the Landlord and Tenant Act.

Compulsory purchase

Inland Revenue *Statement of Practice* SP 8/79 states that any element of compensation received for loss of profits or to cover revenue expenses such as removal costs and interest, will be treated as a revenue receipt.

Compensation which relates to the premises themselves will, however, constitute a capital receipt, and attract capital gains tax unless the sole practitioner or partners are entitled to claim **roll-over relief** or **retirement relief**.

Compensation under the Landlord and Tenant Act

The case of *Drummond v Austin Brown* [1983] STC 506 involved a solicitor who occupied office premises owned by National

Westminster Bank. The bank required the offices for its own business and therefore gave notice under Part II of the Landlord and Tenant Act 1954. Mr Brown received statutory compensation of £31,384. This was held not to be subject to capital gains tax as no asset had been disposed of as required by TCGA 1992, s 22(1) — the receipt flowed from Mr Brown's statutory rights. However, an amount based on statutory rights but paid early for 'voluntary' vacation of the premises, and without the requisite notice being served under the Landlord and Tenant Act, would be subject to capital gains tax. Care is therefore required in this area.

VAT aspects of compensation

A compensation receipt is not normally treated as a VATable supply where the compensation is paid under the Landlord and Tenant Act 1954. Customs and Excise Notice 742B states:

> Compensation paid by a landlord to a tenant under the terms of the Landlord and Tenant Act 1954 (or the Agricultural Holdings Act 1986) is outside the scope of value added tax if a 'Notice to Quit' under the statutory procedures is served by the landlord and complied with by the tenant. Payments by the landlord in addition to the statutory amount (for example in return for the tenant vacating at an earlier date than allowed by the period of grace given in the 'Notice to Quit') are consideration for a standard-rated supply of services by the tenant. 'Compensation' paid to a tenant following purely voluntary negotiations is consideration for a standard-rated supply of services by the tenant, even if it is calculated on the basis of the statutory provisions.

Appendix 1 — memorandum issued by the Law Society on The Solicitors' Accounts Rules 1991, Part III — interest earned on client accounts

Under this part of the rules ('the deposit interest provisions'), a solicitor who is required to account for interest to a client may do so by either of two methods. He or she may:

(1) Account to the client for the interest earned on the client's money in a separate designated account; or
(2) Pay to the client a sum equivalent to the interest which would have accrued for the benefit of the client if money had been deposited in a separate designated account pursuant to the rules. This will usually follow the deposit of the money in general client deposit account.

These two procedures are referred to as Method A and Method B respectively. The tax position under the Solicitors' Accounts (Deposit Interest) Rules 1988, which operated prior to 1 June 1992, was identical.

Deduction of tax at source

The tax deduction at source rules apply, broadly, to designated client accounts, which, before 6 April 1991, were subject to composite rate tax, eg accounts held for individuals who are ordinarily resident in the UK, and, where held with a building society, clients' accounts on which the society was required to account for a sum representing basic rate tax, eg investments by companies, discretionary and accumulation trusts.

Interest on general client accounts, whether with a bank or (since 6 February 1989) a building society, is paid gross.

When opening any designated account the solicitor must provide the necessary information for the bank or building society to decide whether or not deduction of tax at source is appropriate.

Tax treatment of interest — Method A

Method A applies to designated accounts. Where tax is deducted at source by the bank or building society interest will be received by the solicitor net, and he or she will simply pass it on to the client net — no tax deduction certificate is required. The client, when making his or her tax return, will declare the interest as having been received under deduction of tax, and will only be liable to be assessed in relation to higher rate tax in respect of it (since he or she will have a tax credit for basic rate tax). If the client is for any reason not liable to income tax, he or she can recover any tax deducted from the interest. In those circumstances the solicitor must, on being required by the client, obtain a certificate of deduction of tax from the bank or building society and deliver this to the client. The client's position is, therefore, for practical purposes, the same as that which arises where he or she receives interest from a building society or bank on a deposit of his or her own.

Where the client is not liable to tax or is not ordinarily resident in the UK the bank or building society will pay the interest gross provided that it holds the relevant declaration. Declarations of non-ordinary residence can be completed by either the solicitor or the client but declarations of non-liability by UK residents will normally be completed by the client. However, in view of the difficulty of obtaining complete information about an overseas client, solicitors may feel that it is more appropriate for the client concerned to make the declaration, especially since it contains an undertaking to notify the bank or building society should circumstances change.

Where the tax deduction at source rules do not apply, the solicitor will receive interest from the bank or building society gross and may account to the client for it gross, even if the client is non-resident. The client will be assessed on the gross receipt (but a non-resident client may, by concession, not be assessed) and, (unless the solicitor has been acting as the client's agent for tax purposes — see below under 'Solicitors as agents'), the solicitor himself or herself will not be assessed in respect of the interest.

Tax treatment of interest — Method B

Where Method B is used, deduction of tax at source does not apply to the solicitor's general client deposit account at either a bank or building society, and interest is therefore paid to the solicitor gross. When making a payment to the client of an equivalent sum under the deposit interest provisions the solicitor should make the payment gross even if the client is not ordinarily resident. The payment is of compensation in lieu of interest, and is not itself interest. The client will be assessed to income tax on his or her receipt, but a non-resident may, by concession, not be assessed.

Wherever payments are made by solicitors to clients under

Method B they can, in practice, be set off against the solicitor's Case III assessment on gross interest received on general client account deposits; if the payments exceed the interest received, a Case II deduction can be claimed for the excess.

Stake money (position from 1 June 1992)

Under the Solicitors' Accounts Rules 1991 (which came into force on 1 June 1992) stake money is expressly brought within the definition of 'client's money'. Interest will be payable to the person to whom the stake is paid using either Method A or B above. But there will still be circumstances in which payment is not possible until a later tax year. Where this situation looks likely to arise, eg if the stake is held pending the outcome of litigation, the deposit would normally be placed in a general client account until it is established to whom the stake is to be paid. Because, in the meantime, interest will be included in the solicitor's Case III assessment it is again important to make provision for the tax liability to be met out of the interest as it arises.

Tax treatment of interest — money paid into court

The position of monies paid into court is covered by the Supreme Court Funds Rules as amended. Where any order for payment out of monies in court is made, the order should provide for the disposal of any interest accrued to the date of the judgment or order, and for interest accruing thereafter up to the date the monies are paid out in accordance with the order. In the absence of such provision interest accruing between the date of the payment into court, and its acceptance or the judgment or order for payment out, goes to the party who made the payment in, and interest from the date of the judgment or order follows the capital payment.

Where interest is paid to a party to proceedings in respect of money held in court, it should be paid to the client gross, even if he or she is non-resident. The client will normally be assessable under Case III, but the solicitor will not, unless exceptionally he or she is assessable as the client's agents.

Solicitors as agents

Where a solicitor acts for tax purposes as agent for a non-resident client, the solicitor will remain liable to be assessed on behalf of the client in relation to interest earned in a designated deposit account, where Method A is used, unless he or she is an agent without management or control of the interest, in which case, under Extra Statutory Concession B13, no assessment will be made on him or her. Where the solicitor is assessable, the charge may, if appropriate, be to higher rate tax, so the solicitor will need to retain tax at the client's marginal rate of income tax from interest received gross from a bank or building society before remitting it to the client. This is the case even though the account would not be subject to deduction of tax at source since the client would have completed a declaration of non-liability due to his or her non-residence. No question of the solicitor being taxed as an agent will arise where the interest in question has been earned in a general client deposit account, or on stake money, but it could very exceptionally do so in relation to money held in court.

Determination of whether a solicitor has management or control for the purposes of the extra statutory concession will depend on the nature of the solicitor's relationship with the client. Under s 78 of the Taxes Management Act 1970, a person not resident in the United Kingdom is assessable and chargeable to income tax in the name of an agent if the agent has management or control of the interest. Acting as a solicitor in giving advice or in conducting a transaction on the client's instructions will not of itself give management or control nor usually would the holding of a power of attorney on behalf of the client for a specific purpose, eg concluding a specified purchase or sale.

If a client has no fixed place of business in the UK, and his or her solicitor had, and habitually exercised, an authority to conclude contracts on behalf of the client, this would give rise to the client having a permanent establishment in the UK, and accordingly the client would be taxable. In essence, the solicitor would be deemed to have management and control if he or she were effectively carrying on the client's business in the UK, rather than merely acting as a solicitor, even regularly. Therefore, in order for the agency principle to apply, the solicitor/client relationship would normally have to go beyond a solicitor's usual representative capacity. It should be noted that where interest arises in connection with the receipt of rents on behalf of the non-resident, the solicitor would be chargeable as agent in relation to the rent.

If a solicitor is assessable on behalf of the client, he or she has a general right to reimbursement, out of the monies of the client coming into his or her hands, for any tax for which the client is liable and in respect of which the solicitor has been charged.

For the exercise of this right see ss 82 and 84 of the Taxes Management Act 1970.

Trusts

Deduction of tax at source may apply depending upon the type of trust and where the investment is held. But it can only apply where money is held in a designated account. The income of trusts where none of the beneficiaries is ordinarily resident in the UK will not be subject to deduction of tax at source, even if a designated account is used, provided that the appropriate declaration has been made.

Administration of estates

Interest on money held for UK resident personal representatives will, if placed in a designated account, be subject to deduction of tax at source unless a declaration is made by the solicitor or the personal representatives that the deceased was not resident in the UK, immediately before his death.

Type of account	Payment of interest by bank or building society	Consequences
A Designated — where subject to tax deduction.	Net	Pay net to client, who gets basic rate tax credit. No further tax deductions for residents (unless solicitor is assessable as an agent).
B Designated — where paid gross (client money generally).	Gross	Pay gross to client who is assessable on payment as gross income. No deduction of tax for non-residents (unless the solicitor is assessable as agent).
C Bank and building society general client account deposit — always paid gross (client money generally and stake money).	Gross	Pay gross to client who in turn is assessable on payment as gross income; in practice solicitor assessed on interest after setting-off this payment. No deduction of tax for non-residents.

Part III

Tax and the growth of the firm

In this section, we look at the development of a firm from the time that a sole practitioner starts in business, to admitting partners and on to a merger with another firm. We pick out tax considerations which are especially relevant to each phase in the cycle.

Chapter 9

Starting a Practice

In this chapter, we look at some of the key taxation aspects of becoming a sole practitioner

- Practical aspects
- Employment of staff and PAYE compliance
- Pre-trading expenses
- Using your car for business
- Accounts must be produced on the 'earnings basis'
- Choice of accounting date
- Loss relief
- Buying an existing practice

Practical aspects

Recovery of PAYE

If you have been an employed solicitor until now, and you are embarking on self-employment for the first time, bear in mind that the Inland Revenue will often make a repayment of some or all of the tax that you have suffered under PAYE for the year in which you commence practice. Income tax, after all, is an annual tax and the usual practice of the Revenue is to compute the tax payable as if the Schedule E income were the only income for the year — ie set a full year's allowances against the income — and repay any surplus tax withheld under PAYE. This leaves the position clean and ready for the Revenue to issue a Schedule D assessment in due course on the basis that your Schedule D profits are the top slice of your income.

Notifying your local tax district

When you notify the Inspector of Taxes that you have started a practice, you will probably be sent a form 41G (see appendix 1 to this chapter). The Revenue need this basic information so that they can issue returns and notice to self-assessment.

National insurance contributions

As a self-employed person, you will need to pay Class 2 National Insurance Contributions. These can be paid monthly or quarterly.

In due course, once the Inspector receives accounts and agrees your profits, there may well be a further liability for National Insurance, Class 4 contributions. These are currently charged at 7.3 per cent on your taxable profits within the band £6,490–£22,360.

Value Added Tax

It may well be that you will also need to register for VAT. At present, you should apply for registration if you expect your turnover (ie fees) to exceed £45,000 over the first twelve months.

It is possible to use the **cash accounting scheme** if your turnover does not exceed £350,000 per annum. This means that you will need to account for VAT only when your fees are paid. However, bear in mind that if you adopt cash accounting, you will be able to claim input tax on your purchases only for the quarter in which you actually make payment to your suppliers.

Employment of staff and PAYE compliance

It is important that a PAYE Scheme is established from the outset to cover payments to employees. The first step is to contact your local tax district to ascertain the PAYE tax district which covers your practice address. You should then contact that district requesting that a PAYE Scheme be set up. Give an indication to the Inland Revenue of the number of employees likely to be involved.

If a PAYE Scheme is not in place by the first pay date, you should make provisional deductions pending receipt of a PAYE reference.

PAYE deductions made by an employer must normally be paid to the Collector of Taxes within 14 days from the end of each tax month. However, it is possible to take advantage of a scheme for small employers if you believe that the average monthly payments of PAYE and National Insurance Contributions are likely to be less than £450 per month. Employers who come within this category can account for PAYE and National Insurance Contributions on a quarterly basis.

Pre-trading expenses

If an expense is incurred in setting up a practice, but before it commences business, tax relief is due. The expenses are treated as a loss incurred in the year that the solicitor opens for business.
Examples of common types of pre-trading expenses are:

- Incidental costs of raising loan finance;
- Bank charges and bank interest;
- Rent for business premises;
- Other expenses related to business premises such as rates, heating and lighting;
- Leasing costs of plant, machinery, or office equipment and similar items;
- insurance;
- Printing and stationery;
- Advertising;
- Wages or other remuneration of employees; and
- Accountancy fees.

Pre-trading expenditure which qualifies for capital allowances is dealt with rather differently in that. The expenditure is normally treated as having been incurred at the time that the practice opens for business.

Using your car for business

A sole practitioner may claim a proportion of his running costs, and capital allowances, where he uses his car for business.

A special rule applies where a sole practitioner uses his car which until now has been used only for private purposes. The legislation provides that capital allowances are due only on the market value at the time that it is brought into use for the firm. In practice the Revenue normally take the market value as equal to the original cost less notional writing-down allowances for the period of ownership before the business commenced.

EXAMPLE

Andrew buys a motor car in 1993 for £10,000 and used it privately for 12 months before bringing it into use for a new business. He is able to claim capital allowances only on a notional acquisition cost of £7,500. This is computed by reference to the capital allowances which would have been due for the first 12 months of ownership if he had been using it for the business in that period. In other words:

	£
Cost	10,000
Less notional writing-down allowance	2,500
	7,500

Accounts must be produced on the earnings basis

The Revenue's view is that accounts should normally be prepared so as to include a practitioners earnings for a year rather than just the cash actually received. This means that the accounts should include debtors, ie bills which have been issued but which have not been paid by the year end. Similarly, the accounts should include work in progress (but not your own time costs — see p 75).

The Revenue will normally require accounts to be prepared on the earnings basis for the first three years of a business. Thereafter, the Revenue will allow a firm to switch to a cash basis, or to a bills delivered basis, provided the firm gives an undertaking that invoices will be issued at regular and frequent intervals once work has been completed (see Inland Revenue Statement of Practice A27 — appendix 2 to this chapter).

Where accounts are prepared on the cash basis, expenses must also be accounted for on the cash basis, ie if an invoice has not been paid by the year end it is not a deductible expense until the year in which it is paid.

Choice of accounting date

In general, a solicitor who starts a practice will need to survive an initial period in which a great deal of setting-up costs are incurred — and often there is relatively little fee income coming in. Once this phase is over, cash flow is likely to be more healthy.

Assuming that a newly formed practice follows this pattern, there is a lot to be said for drawing up the first accounts for a 12 month period, since this will tend to defer tax.

EXAMPLE

Charles starts up in practice on 1 January 1995. His management accounts show profits as follows:

	£
1 January–31 March 1995	2,000
1 April–31 December 1995	27,000
1 January–31 March 1996	10,000
1 April–30 April 1996	3,000
1 May–31 December 1996	25,000
1 January–31 March 1997	12,000

If Charles makes up accounts for the first 12 months, the position will be:

Assessable		£
1994/95	$3/_{12}$ × £29,000 =	7,250
1995/96	First 12 months =	29,000
1996/97	Year ended 31 December 1996	38,000

In contrast, a 31 March year end will produce assessments as follows:

Assessable		£
1994/95	Period ended 31 March 1995	2,000
1995/96	Year ended 31 March 1996	37,000
1996/97	Year ended 31 March 1997	40,000

If the first accounts are for a period of 15 months, the position will be:

Assessable		£
1994/95	$\frac{3}{15}$ × £39,000	7,800
1995/96	$\frac{12}{15}$ × £39,000	31,200
1996/97	Year ended 31 March 1997	40,000

Over the entire life of the practice, things will even out — because of **overlap relief**. However, it will normally be desired to keep tax (and class 4 NIC) down to the very minimum in the early years.

It must be recognised, however, that tax planning is not the only aspect to be borne in mind. Other considerations may lead a practitioner to select an accounting date which avoids any periods of seasonal pressure and which fits in with the bank's requirements for accounts.

Loss relief

A solicitor in practice may make a loss at any stage in his career, but it is more likely that losses will arise whilst the practice is in its infancy.

Relief may be taken for such losses in various different ways. In general, the taxpayer must notify the Revenue within two years if the loss is to be set against other income (see below).

Carry back relief

Where a loss is incurred during one of the first four tax years in which a solicitor has been engaged in carrying on the practice, relief may be claimed under ICTA 1988, s 381. This section permits losses to be carried back against the individual's income for the preceding three tax years. The loss is carried back and relieved against the earliest year first — this will normally produce the maximum repayment supplement on any repayment.

EXAMPLE

John starts in practice on 1 May 1993. Accounts are prepared to 31 March 1994 showing a loss of £20,000. This is a loss for the tax year 1993/94 and it can be carried back and relieved against John's income for the year

1990/91, with any balance of unrelieved losses then being relieved against his 1991/92 and 1992/93 income.

Set-off against other income for year of loss

Losses can also be relieved against an individual's other income for the year of loss. Alternatively, it is possible to claim for the loss to be relieved against income for the following tax year (provided the profession is being carried on in that year). This is to be changed under the new system, to allow relief for the loss to be claimed against income of the preceding year. This change will take effect for losses incurred in 1997/98 and subsequent years.

EXAMPLE

James has been in practice for many years and incurs a loss for the accounts year ended 31 March 1994. The loss is for the year 1993/94 and can be relieved either:

(a) against James's income for 1993/94 or/and

(b) against James's income for 1994/95.

If the loss had been for a year after 1996/97 alternative (b) would instead permit the loss to be set against James's income for the preceding year.

The alternatives (a) and (b) can be claimed in any order, ie (b) first with any balance against income stated in (a), or the reverse, or one claim may be made in isolation.

In looking at the income against which a loss may be set, consideration should be given to any capital gains. A claim to set a loss against other income can be extended so that any loss which remains unutilised may be set against any capital gains for the tax year of the loss, or, once again, gains of the following tax year. However, it is not possible to confine a loss claim to the amount of the individual's capital gains, a loss must be first set against an individual's income.

Concessional basis

Relief for losses is normally given by reference to the loss arising for an accounting period. Strictly, losses should be calculated for a tax year, but this is normally only adhered to during the opening three tax years and the closing years.

EXAMPLE

Mark has Schedule D Case II profits/losses as follows:

	£
Year ended 30 April 1993	10,000
Year ended 30 April 1994	(20,000)

Under the concessional basis, Mark has a loss for 1994/95 of £20,000. Under the strict basis, he has a loss for 1993/94 of:

	£
$\frac{1}{12}$ × £10,000 =	833
$\frac{11}{12}$ × (£20,000) =	(18,333)
	(17,500)

A taxpayer may, if it is advantageous, elect for losses to be calculated on strict basis. However, it is not possible to switch and chose each year between the two bases as once a loss has been claimed under the strict basis, the following year's loss (if any) must be calculated under the same basis.

Other types of loss relief

Relief may sometimes be secured 'by aggregation' ie a loss is set against a profit of another period in arriving at the profits of the first 12 months' trading. Thus, if Paul started to practice on 1 January 1994 and made a loss of £20,000 for the four months ended 30 April 1994 and a profit for the following 12 months of £24,000 relief by aggregation would mean that the first 12 months would be taken as a loss of £4,000, ie:

	£
loss for period ended 30 April 1994	(20,000)
$\frac{8}{12}$ of profit for year ended 30 April 1995	16,000
	(4,000)

Relief by aggregation can sometimes be the most beneficial method, but it is not possible to secure relief twice.

Carry forward relief

If no other claim is possible, the loss can always be carried forward for relief against future Schedule D Case II profits. This loss relief can be carried forward indefinitely, but may be lost if the activity ceases, even though a similar business may be commenced subsequently.

Terminal loss relief

A special type of loss relief is available for losses made in the 12 months prior to an individual ceasing to carrying on a profession. We deal with this at p 184.

Buying an existing practice

Where a solicitor purchases a practice, the amount paid must be broken down into payments for separate assets such as goodwill, office premises, fixtures and fittings etc.

A lump sum payment may well include a capital payment for goodwill. There is no income tax relief for such expenditure, although it is possible that capital gains tax **roll-over relief** may be obtained. If you have realised a capital gain on the sale of another practice (or, indeed, on the disposal of any business or asset used by a firm in which you were a partner — see pp 91–93).

Similarly, no income tax relief is due for any part of the purchase price which relates to the acquisition of office premises or the assignment of a lease. Once again this is capital expenditure and the most that you can hope for is capital gains tax roll-over relief — If you have made eligible gains.

Fixtures and fittings may include some items which are eligible for capital allowances. In general, you may be able to obtain writing-down allowances based on the amount attributable to qualifying items of plant and machinery.

Value Added Tax

The purchase of an existing practice will normally qualify as a transfer of a going concern for VAT purposes. The effect is that the transfer of assets will not be subject to a VAT charge. Where property is transferred and the vendor has made an election to waive exemption, the purchaser must similarly elect in order for the transfer to qualify for VAT relief.

Planning points

There can be situations where it will be possible to negotiate an arrangement whereby the former proprietor receives an annuity. In general, this is 'tax efficient' for a purchaser since he may secure higher rate income tax relief on the annuity payments.

Conversely, the whole of the annuity will be taxable income for the vendor and capital gains tax reliefs such as retirement relief may go to waste — so this is a situation where what suits the purchaser may not be attractive to the vendor.

In some cases, it may be possible for the purchaser and vendor to practise in partnership together, perhaps for a brief period of three to six months. In most situations, the vendor will have been in practice at 5 April 1994 so an arrangement of this nature may mean that the firm is assessed on the **preceding year basis** for 1995/96 and on the transitional basis for 1996/97.

EXAMPLE

Gerald has been in practice for a number of years. His profits for the year ended 30 April 1994 were £28,000.

Julie wishes to take over the practice and expects to make it more profitable.

If she becomes a partner on 1 February 1995 and Gerald retires on 30 April 1995, and provided a **continuation election** is made, the position will be:

		£
1995/96	PY basis	28,000
1996/97	50 per cent of profits for the period 1 May 1994–30 April 1996	

If Julie succeeds in making the practice more profitable, her actual profits for 1996/97 may be substantially more than her assessment for that year.

This arrangement might also suit Gerald if a cessation would leave him exposed to the Revenue applying the **closing years rules**.

Value Added Tax

Where the vendor is charging VAT on the transfer of assets, it is prudent to ensure that the transfer of going concern provisions do not apply. If Customs & Excise decide that they do apply, the purchaser's recovery of the VAT may be denied.

	Reference

	District date stamp

I understand you may now be self employed (this includes subcontracting in the Construction Industry). If so please let me have the information asked for below and over the page as soon as possible.

If this is the first time you have been self employed, you may find booklet IR28 'Starting in Business' helpful. You can get this from any Tax Enquiry Centre or Tax Office. If you need any further help I shall be pleased to arrange an appointment for you to see me.

When you become self employed, you normally pay National Insurance contributions (Class 2). Please get in touch with your local office of the Contributions Agency (DSS) about this.

Enquiries about yourself and any business partners

Yourself

Your surname

Your first names

Your private address

Postcode _____

Tax Office to which last Income Tax Return made

Reference in that Office

National Insurance number

Date of birth ... ...

Day	Month	Year

Business partners

	Partner 1	Partner 2	Partner 3
Partner's surname			
Partner's first names			
Partner's private address			
	Postcode _____	Postcode _____	Postcode _____

If you have more than three business partners please give the names and addresses of any other partners on a separate sheet

41G(1993)

Please turn over

Enquiries about the business — Replies

1. In what name is the business carried on, if not in your own name?
2. What is the business address, including postcode, if different from your private address? — Postcode
3. What is the nature of the business?
4. When did you start in this business? — 19
5. If you took over an existing business, who did you acquire it from? — Name / Address / Postcode
6. To what date do you propose to make up your business accounts? — 19. If they are to be prepared by a firm of accountants, please give their name and address, including postcode. — Name / Address / Postcode
7. If you are not already operating PAYE as an employer, have you any employees earning
   - more than £66.50 a week or £288 a month?
   - more than £1 a week who have other employment?

   Yes ☐ No ☐ — *please tick '✓' appropriate box.*

Personal enquiries — Replies

8. Were you employed or were you self employed before you started this business? What was the name and address of the business or employer? Please give this information even if you had a period of unemployment between leaving employment and starting your own business.

   Employed ☐ Self employed ☐ *tick '✓' one box*
   Name / Address / Postcode

   If you still have the leaving certificate form P45 handed to you by your last employer, please attach it and give the leaving date. — 19
9. If this is your first occupation since leaving full time education on what date did the education finish? — 19
10. If as well as running your business you are in paid employment, or are continuing an existing business, please give the name and address of the employer/existing business. — Name / Address / Postcode

    Is this an existing business or employment? — Existing business ☐ Employment ☐ *tick '✓' one box*

Signature — Date — 19

Please say whether you are single, married, widowed, separated or divorced

Appendix 1 — Inland Revenue Statement of Practice A27: accounts prepared on a cash basis

A company, whether limited or unlimited, is normally required to prepare accounts for tax purposes on an earnings basis, as defined in [ICTA 1988, s 110]. An individual or a partnership carrying on a trade is similarly required to prepare accounts on an earnings basis, but in the circumstances set out below accounts prepared on a cash basis, or on a conventional basis such as bills issued or work completed which is neither full 'earnings' nor pure 'cash', may be accepted from an individual or partnership carrying on a profession or vocation.

Where a profession or vocation is newly set up, or is treated as new for tax purposes (as under [ICTA 1988, s 113(1)]), the profits of the first three years from the date of setting up or of the change to which [ICTA 1988, s 113(1)] applies are required to be computed on the earnings basis (as defined in [ICTA 1988, s 110(3)] in determining all tax liabilities affected by the profits of these years.

The computation of subsequent profits will continue on the earnings basis until the taxpayer asks to change to a cash or other conventional basis. Such a basis will be accepted if the new basis seems likely to provide a reasonable measure of the taxpayer's profit. This is interpreted as meaning that the profits computed on the new basis will not, taking one year with another, differ materially from the profits computed on the earnings basis.

The change must also be a complete one. For example, receipts after the change for work done before the change must be brought into the computation of profits on the cash basis notwithstanding that they have already been brought into account in the computation on the earnings basis; similarly, expenses accrued due but unpaid which were debited in the accounts on the earnings basis may again be debited in the subsequent accounts on the cash basis when they are paid.

A further condition is that the taxpayer wishing to make such a change is required to give a written undertaking that he will issue bills for services rendered or work done (that is in the normal way, completed work but also including work in progress where interim payments or payments on account are contemplated by the terms of the contract or are customary) at regular and frequent intervals. The intervals may be chosen by the taxpayer but they should be quarterly or more often, and they should be specified in the undertaking.

Attention is drawn to the possibility of liability under [ICTA 1988, s 104], wherever accounts are prepared on a basis other than earnings: in computing such liability there is no provision for any relief in respect of any profits which may have been brought into the computation twice when the change from the earnings basis was made.

Where accounts are prepared on a cash or other conventional basis and it is desired to change to an earnings basis, no objection will be raised but attention is again drawn to the liability that will arise under [ICTA 1988, s 104]. A subsequent claim to revert to a conventional basis would not be accepted.

Chapter 10

Admitting a partner

In this chapter, we look at various aspects from the perspective of a sole practitioner who is considering taking someone into partnership.

- Introduction.
- Continuation election.
- Partnership capital requirements — and funding.
- Interest on capital.
- Provision of cars.
- Capital gains tax considerations.
- Keeping certain property assets outside the firm.
- Compliance matters.
- Admitting a partner under the new rules.

Introduction

We are basically working on the assumption that the typical firm will have been in existence on 5 April 1994 and is at present taxed on the **PY basis**. The last section of this chapter deals with situations where this is not the case and the firm is already being assessed on the CY basis.

We are also assuming that the new partner will be a full partner assessed under Schedule D, and not a **salaried partner** assessed under Schedule E. No significant tax consequences apply for the firm if a salaried partner is admitted as for tax purposes the individual is treated as a senior employee.

Continuation election

The introduction of a partner before 6 April 1997 may give rise to a **cessation** of the 'old' firm unless a **continuation election** is made. The closing years' rules may apply if there is a cessation (see Chapter 2) and the new firm will be dealt with under the CY basis and the new Schedule D regime.

There may well be useful tax savings to be achieved by making a continuation election. This will in general preserve the preceding year basis assessment for 1995/96 and prevent the Revenue making increased assessments for the two tax years before the admittance of the partner. It should also ensure that 1996/97 is assessed under the **transitional year basis rules**. Indeed, the elevation of a senior employee or the introduction of a partner who will generate additional fees should often maximise the benefits of the transitional rules for 1996/97.

EXAMPLE

Philip is a sole practitioner. His taxable profits have been as follows:

	£
Year ended 30 April 1992	35,000
Year ended 30 April 1993	38,000
Year ended 30 April 1994	45,000
Year ended 30 April 1995	52,000

He admits Robin as a partner on 1 May 1995. The firm's assessments have been as follows:

		£
1993/94	PY basis	35,000
1994/95	PY basis	38,000
1995/96	PY basis	45,000

If Robin joins in a continuation election, these assessments will not be disturbed. Furthermore, if the profits for the year ended 30 April 1996 show a substantial increase there will be a further tax saving. Thus, if the profits for the year ended 30 April 1996 are £80,000, the assessment will be on £66,000 (50 per cent of the profits for the two years ended 30 April 1996) and this assessment will be shared between Philip and Robin.

It is, therefore, important that a term of the partnership agreement should be that an in-coming partner will join in a continuation election where requested to do so. It is also important (in case the partnership doesn't work out) that the agreement requires him to join in a continuation election if he should leave the firm before 6 April 1997 and the continuing partner wishes to make such an election.

A continuation election must be submitted within two years of the change in partners. It must be signed by all the parties concerned, ie all the former partners and the individuals who will be partners after the change.

Partners may submit a provisional continuation election which will then stand unless it is formally revoked within the two year period.

There may be situations where a continuation election is not appropriate — perhaps where the firm's business is much less profitable and a cessation will produce a lower assessment for the partners in the on-going firm. Such a cessation may have important consequences, eg accounts will need to be produced on the full **earnings basis**. The partners will be assessed personally and the CY rules will apply. Nevertheless, there will be good aspects as well as draw-backs, eg the principle of joint and several liability for the firm's Schedule D Case II income tax will not apply.

Partnership capital requirements — and funding

One aspect of the partnership agreement which needs to be addressed is the amount of partnership capital required. Where a sole practitioner has carried on his practice for a number of years, borrowings may have been built up on an ad hoc basis and will often consist mainly of a bank overdraft. The admission of a partner is an excellent time to take stock and to put the practice's finances on a better footing by the partners contributing partnership capital. This may also avoid problems in the longer term if one partner has substantially more private wealth as such an individual will be more exposed if the firm operates a steadily increasing overdraft.

A perfectly satisfactory alternative is for partners to take personal loans from their bank and then make a loan to the firm.

Income tax relief is available under ICTA 1988, s 362 for interest on personal loans taken by partners in order to contribute partnership capital, or to make a loan to the firm.

The full requirements of s 362 are:

1)   the loan must not be an overdraft;
2)   the loan must be used to finance a payment of capital into the firm or to finance a loan to the firm for use in its business;
3)   the borrower must not have recovered any capital from the firm — the loan ceases to qualify to the extent that there has been such a recovery.

Not only is it commercially appropriate for partners to borrow in their personal capacity, this may well give rise to useful tax savings during the next few years:

EXAMPLE

Adam admits Louise as a partner on 1 January 1995. They will share profits equally. Until that time, the practice has operated on a 'core' overdraft of £60,000. Profits have been as follows:

	£
Year ended 31 December 1993	55,000
Year ended 31 December 1994	60,000

It is agreed that Adam and Louise will each borrow £30,000 personally and introduce this as partnership capital.

Adam and Louise join in a continuation election.

If we assume interest is paid at ten per cent per annum, and the firm's profits for the years ended 31 December 1995 and 31 December 1996 will be £75,000 and £95,000 respectively, the position will be as follows:

1994/95

Firm's assessable profits — PY basis	£55,000

1995/96

Firm's assessable profits — PY basis		£60,000

divided:	Adam	Louise
	£	£
	30,000	30,000
less interest relief	3,000	3,000
	27,000	27,000

1996/97

Firm's assessable profit — 50 per cent of combined profits of the two years ended 31 December 1996, ie 50 per cent of £170,000 = £85,000

divided:	Adam	Louise
	£	£
	42,500	42,500
less interest relief	3,000	3,000
	39,500	39,500

There is a double benefit. Firstly, the 1995/96 assessment is on a figure which will have been depressed by interest charged on the firm's overdraft during the basis period (year ended 31 December 1994), but Adam and Louise will also receive relief for the interest paid by them during 1995/96. Secondly, Adam and Louise will receive relief for all the interest paid in 1995/96–1996/97 whereas the firm is assessed on only 50 per cent of its profits for the two year **transitional year basis period**.

There may be a concern that anti-avoidance legislation may apply where partners in a firm replace a 'core' overdraft by introducing capital funded by personal loans — see p 45. However, it is unlikely that this legislation (details of which will not be available until the publication of the 1995 Finance Bill) will apply to a situation where a sole practitioner admits a partner.

It is also likely that a partner's **transitional** relief will be higher if the firm is financed by partners' capital/loans rather than bank borrowings. Basically, transitional relief relates to the proportion of the profits assessable for 1997/98 which are earned during the period up to 5 April 1997.

EXAMPLE

Jonathan is a partner in a firm with a 30 April year end. His share of the profits for the year ended 30 April 1997 is £73,000.

He will be assessed on £73,000 for 1997/98. However, an amount equal to:

$$\frac{\text{1 May 1996 - 5 April 1997}}{\text{1 May 1996 - 30 April 1997}} \times £73,000$$

will be allowed as a deduction for the year in which he ceases to be a partner (or in some circumstances the year in which the firm changes its accounting date).

The transitional relief will be $^{340}/_{365} \times £73,000$ ie £68,000

If Jonathan and his partners had financed the firm by partnership capital the profits for the year ended 30 April 1997 would be greater by the amount of the interest paid personally by the partners. The position for 1997/98 would have been as follows:

	£
Profits for the year ended 30 April 1997	90,000
less relief for interest paid personally (say)	17,000
Net amount on which Jonathan is assessed	73,000

The net amount assessable is unchanged and the partner's tax liability for 1997/98 is thus unaffected. However, it appears from the legislation as so far enacted that Jonathan's transitional relief would then be $^{340}/_{365} \times$ **£90,000** ie £83,835 because transitional relief is based on the firm's profit rather than on the net sum on which the partner bears tax.

Interest on capital

It will generally be appropriate for interest to be paid on partners' capital accounts, especially where there is some disparity between the amounts of capital provided by each partner.

'Interest' paid in these circumstances is treated as an allocation of Schedule D Case II profits rather than as interest taxable under Schedule D Case III. This has the effect that the partner's **relevant earnings** for personal pension purposes are likely to be higher than if the firm borrows from a bank to meet its working capital requirements.

EXAMPLE

Anthony is a sole practitioner. His profits are running at the rate of £50,000 per annum.

He brings in a partner and finances the practice by a loan which he raises in his personal capacity.

At the end of the year, his position may be:

	£
Interest on capital	12,000
Share of profits	50,000
Interest paid on personal borrowings	(10,000)
	52,000

However, for personal pension purposes, his relevant earnings are £62,000 — ie no deduction for interest relieved under ICTA 1988, s 362.

Provision of cars

Where a partner uses his own car for the practice's business, he is entitled to capital allowances. If he has bought his car by taking a bank loan, he may also be entitled to relief for interest by him.

Capital allowances

The partner will be entitled to a proportion of the capital allowances which would be available if the car were used only for business purposes.

EXAMPLE

Marilyn is in a firm which makes up accounts to 31 August. She uses her car 75 per cent for personal use, 25 per cent for business. She paid £14,000 for the car in June 1993.

Her capital allowances for 1994/95 will normally be:

Maximum allowance	3,000	
less restriction for private use	2,250	
allowances due 1994/95	750	(PY basis)

Loan interest

Relief is available for interest paid on a loan used to buy a car (or other item of plant and machinery such as a photocopier or fax machine kept at home). Interest is eligible for relief only if it is paid within three tax years following the year in which the car is purchased.

EXAMPLE

If in the above example, Marilyn had borrowed £10,000 to buy her car, she would be entitled to relief on 25 per cent of the interest paid during the period 1993/94–1996/97.

No relief is due if the 'loan' is in fact a standard HP agreement as interest on such an agreement is not true annual interest for tax purposes. Interest is allowed as a charge against the individual's income for the year in which it is paid even though the Schedule D Case II assessment may be made on the PY basis.

Capital gains tax considerations

There will normally be no capital gains tax charge if a sole practitioner and his new partner each put in new capital on an equal basis — or in proportion to their profit-sharing ratios. However, it is possible that a sole practitioner may require the incoming partner to put in capital on the basis that this simply matches the value of his interest in the firm. The normal way to account for this is to re-value goodwill and this could give rise to a capital gain.

EXAMPLE

Steve brings Catherine into partnership, sharing profits equally. Catherine is required to pay £50,000 capital into the firm, but Steve will not need to pay any money into the firm, and, indeed, will be free to withdraw all his undrawn profits. On the other hand, it is agreed that half of the goodwill now belongs to Catherine.

A situation like this really amounts to an agreement that Steve's goodwill is worth £50,000. After admitting Catherine as a partner, he is entitled to only half of this but he is also entitled to half of the £50,000 cash that she has put into the firm. So, in effect Steve has received a capital payment for a disposal of half of the goodwill and there may be a capital gains tax charge on this.

The exceptions to the normal rules described in Chapter 7 should also be borne in mind if you will receive a cash payment to admit a partner or if the incoming partner is a relative (ie a connected person).

Keeping certain property assets outside the firm

It may well be that a sole practitioner wishes to retain full personal ownership of the office premises etc, and does not wish to share them with the incoming partners. This problem may be more apparent than real since there is no requirement that partners should share capital profits in the same ways as they share ordinary profits. Nevertheless, many people will prefer to keep the premises outside the firm altogether.

In such a situation the former sole practitioner can rent the premises to the firm, preferably under formal agreement which gives the firm a tenancy or a licence. He can also charge rent although the long term effect on capital gains tax retirement relief should be borne in mind (see p 189).

Any rent charged will normally be exempt from VAT and VAT on related costs may therefore be irrecoverable. If substantial costs are incurred, the partner may **elect to waive exemption** and charge VAT on the rent. Care is needed before making such an election as it is irrevocable.

It is also possible for the partner to forgo rent, but to receive an appropriate adjustment in the partnership accounts, as a prior charge on profits in the same way as interest on capital. If the partnership agreement is drafted correctly, this will effectively convert Schedule A rental income for the partner into profits falling under Schedule D Case II.

Compliance matters

A VAT registered sole practitioner who brings someone into partnership is required to notify Customs & Excise. Under VAT legislation, a partnership is treated as a taxable person. The partners are jointly and severally liable for VAT.

Provided the sole practitioner is not retaining part of the practice in his own name, his VAT registration will be cancelled. The partnership will either be given a new registration number or the sole practitioner's number can be transferred to the partnership. Where the latter course is adopted, the firm takes over liability for all VAT liabilities of the sole practitioner.

Admitting a partner under the new rules

Matters are much more straightforward in a situation where the firm is already on the CY basis, either because the business was started after 5 April 1994 or because a partner retired from the firm after that date and no continuation election has been (or will be) made.

Basically, the partnership's profits will be assessed on the CY basis (bear in mind the opening rules — see p 4). Each partner will be separately responsible for settling his own tax, there will be no principle of joint and several liability for the firm's income tax.

Once the new rules apply to the firm, any subsequent changes in the partners will not give rise to a cessation. Indeed, under the new rules there will be an automatic 'continuation'. A cessation will occur only if all the partners cease to carry on the business.

Thus, on a partnership change under the new rules, the tax liabilities of existing partners are not affected because the change does not trigger a Revenue review of tax assessments for the penultimate and ante-penultimate years.

Appendix 1 — Statement of Practice SP4/85: Relief for interest on loans used to buy property occupied by a partnership

1. Under [ICTA 1988, s 355(1)(*b*) and (4)] an individual who pays interest on a loan he has taken out to buy land which is commercially let can obtain relief for the interest paid by setting it against his letting income. The land has to be let at a commercial rent for more than 26 weeks in any 52 week period which includes the time at which the interest is payable and, when not so let, it has to be available for such letting, or used as the owner's only or main residence, or unavailable because it is undergoing repairs.

2. Where therefore an individual pays interest on a loan to buy a property which is let for business purposes to a partnership of which he is a member, he will generally be able to set the interest payable against rent received from the partnership, and the rent paid will be eligible for relief as a business expense in computing the partnership profits.

3. Property owned by a partner is sometimes occupied rent-free by the partnership, and in practice a deduction has been allowed against the partnership's profits where the partnership pays the interest direct on behalf of the partner, or even, in some cases, where the partnership makes no payment of interest or rent at all. More recently the question has been raised of extending this practice to similar circumstances where property, which is owned by a director with a controlling interest in a company, is occupied rent-free for business purposes by that company.

4. The Revenue have been reviewing their practice in this area, and have concluded that in some respect it goes further than is justified by the relevant legislation. They now propose to apply the provisions as follows.

5. Where land owned by an individual partner is occupied for the purposes of a profession by the partnership, and the interest on the loan (other than an overdraft) taken out by the partner to purchase the land is paid by the partnership and charged in its accounts, the payment will be regarded

as a rent for the use of the land. It will thus be eligible to be treated as an allowable expense in computing the partnership profits. It will be taxable as rent in the hands of the individual partner, but will be regarded as covered by the interest for which he is liable and which will qualify for relief under [TA 1988 s 355(1)(*b*),(4) ICTA 1988] if the conditions of [s 355(1)(*b*)] are met. The payment will also be regarded as rent payable by the partnership to the individual partner in the calculation of any CGT relief available to him.

6. Where no payment of rent or interest is made by the partnership, no deduction will be allowed in computing the partnership profits for the interest paid by the partner himself. But as the land is occupied rent-free, CGT retirement relief would not be restricted by reference to any rent payable.

Chapter 11

Becoming a partner

This chapter looks at matters more from the in-coming partner's point of view.

- Salaried partner or Schedule D partner?
- Joint and several liability for tax.
- Basis of assessment.
- Qualifying loans.
- Loss relief.
- Capital gains tax aspects.

Salaried partner or Schedule D partner?

An individual may be held out to the world at large as a partner, and may thereby become exposed to potential claims which may fall on a partner, and yet still be an employee in the eyes of the Inland Revenue. If there is a master/servant relationship and he does not take part in the management of the business, he is still an employee. This will mean that his remuneration is charged to tax under Schedule E and PAYE should be withheld.

Joint and several liability for tax

The principle of joint and several liability for the firm's tax liabilities will not apply in relation to 1997/98 and subsequent years. If you join a firm between now and 6 April 1997, you may make yourself jointly liable for tax on profits earned after your admission — this will depend upon whether you join in a **continuation election**. If you do join in such an election, you will be jointly and severally liable for tax until the introduction of the new CY basis. If you do not enter into a continuation election, the firm will be regarded as having a cessation on your admission to the partnership and a new firm as having been brought into being. Each partner in the new firm will be personally liable for the tax on his share of the profits. If you do agree to join a continuation election, you should seek an indemnity so that if any additional tax is payable by you, over and above the tax you would have suffered if there had been a cessation, it will be reimbursed by the partners who benefit from the continuation election.

Basis of assessment

The position here will be affected quite fundamentally by the Finance Act 1994 and the new rules on Schedule D basis of assessment.

If you become a partner in a firm which is already on the CY basis, either because the firm was started after 5 April 1994 or because there has already been a change in partners and no continuation election will be made, you will be assessed separately on your share of the profits. The basis of assessment will be as set out in Chapter 1, ie for the first tax year in which you are a partner you will be assessed on your actual profits for that year. For the second tax year in which you are a partner, you will normally be assessed on your share of profits earned in the first 12 months. In year 3, you will move on to the CY basis.

In contrast to the above, if you join an existing firm which is presently taxed under the PY basis, and a continuation election is made, you will be taxed on your share of the profits which are assessed on the firm for each tax year up to 1996/97 and from 1997/98 onwards you will move on to the CY basis.

If you are admitted as a partner in 1996/97, there may be a slightly strange situation whereby the basis on which you are assessed for 1997/98 may be different from that which applies to your partners.

EXAMPLE

Phillipa becomes a partner on 1 November 1996. The firm makes up accounts to 30 April.

Phillipa will be assessed for 1996/97 on her share of the firm's assessment. For 1997/98, she will be assessed on her profits for the first 12 months, ie:

$^6/_{12}$ × profits for year ended 30 April 1997.

plus $^6/_{12}$ × profits for year ended 30 April 1998.

Phillipa's partners will simply be assessed for 1997/98 on their share of the firm's profits for the year ended 30 April 1997.

Qualifying loans

Section 362 of ICTA 1988 enables an individual to secure income tax relief in respect of interest paid during a tax year on a loan which has been used in order to finance the introduction of partnership capital or where the borrowed money has itself been lent on to the firm for use in the firm's business. There is an overriding requirement that the individual must not be a limited partner, but must be involved in the management of the firm's business.

In theory, problems could arise where the partner's loan is secured against his main residence which is owned jointly. However, Inland Revenue Savings and Investment Division confirmed some years ago that where the interest is paid by the spouse who is in the partnership, the interest qualifies for relief notwithstanding that the loan is secured on a property which is owned jointly with a non partner.

Even if the interest is paid out of a joint bank account, the Inland Revenue do not normally seek to restrict relief provided that it can be shown that the interest is actually borne by the partner rather than by his spouse.

Restriction on relief

A loan ceases to qualify for relief under s 362 to the extent that the individual recovers capital from the firm. This could cause problems if your drawings exceed your share of profits during the early years.

Salaried partners

If you are a salaried partner, but are required to put in capital, the following *Statement of Practice* should be borne in mind:

Relief for interest payments: loans applied in acquiring an interest in a partnership

The Board are advised that s 362 ICTA 1988 extend[s] to salaried partners in a professional firm who are allowed independence of action in handling the affairs of clients and generally so to act that they will be indistinguishable from general partners in their relations with clients.

Loss relief

A partner's share of any losses are eligible for relief in the same way as a sole practitioner's losses — ie by being carried forward to cover profits from the firm in subsequent years or by set-off against the partner's general income for the year of the loss, or (up to 1996/97) by set-off against the partner's general income for the following tax year (provided the partner is with the firm at some time during the following year). Furthermore, an individual may carry back losses incurred during the first four years of his being a partner — such losses are carried back against the individual's general income of the three tax years preceding the year of loss, taking the earliest year first.

For further details of the treatment of losses, see Chapter 8.

There is one aspect of partnership losses which can be confusing. Any adjustments for partners' interest and partners' salaries need to be added back, and it is only the remaining amount of any losses which can be relieved.

EXAMPLE

Helen is a partner in a five partner firm.

The firm's accounts show a loss of £10,000.

However, on further investigation this turns out to be computed as follows:

	£
Profits	100,000
Less interest on partners' capital accounts	(30,000)
	70,000
Less partners' salaries	(80,000)
Loss per accounts	(10,000)

Because interest on partners' capital accounts and partners' salaries are treated as an allocation of profits, as opposed to a deduction in arriving at those profits, there is no loss for tax purposes, but rather income of £100,000 to be allocated amongst the partners.

Similarly, if a partner guarantees a 'salary' to one of his colleagues, this cannot create a loss situation. Thus, if Helen had guaranteed a salary to one of her colleagues of £30,000 (in addition to the partners' salaries already in the accounts), there would be no relief for this whatsoever.

Capital gains tax aspects

An aspect which needs to be borne in mind is that where an individual becomes a partner, he will normally take over the firm's historic acquisition cost of various chargeable assets owned by the firm. The one exception to this is where there is a re-valuation of partnership assets at the time of his becoming a partner (see chapter 7).

Chapter 12

Buying out a partner

In this chapter, we look at some of the tax considerations which apply where a partner is being bought out, either by a number of partners or by just one partner who wishes to take over the whole practice and run it as a sole practitioner.

There are almost infinite different ways of structuring an agreed way of compensating a partner for his agreeing to retire from the firm. The issues most frequently requiring consideration are:

- Gradual withdrawal from the firm.
- Change in status to salaried partner.
- Consultancy arrangement.
- Annuity arrangements.
- Payment of a capital sum.
- Continuation or cessation?
- Splitting the practice.

We look at matters mainly (but not exclusively) from the perspective of the continuing partners.

Gradual withdrawal from the firm

In a situation where relationships are reasonably amicable, the 'buy-out' may consist of an orderly withdrawal from the firm's business with the outgoing partner being allowed a full share of profits for a period of a year or so leading up to his retirement from the firm. For the on-going partners' point of view, they do not have to find any capital payment and from the continuing partner's point of view he benefits since he receives relevant earnings on which he can pay personal pension contributions.

This type of arrangement may also be appropriate where the outgoing partner owns the firm's office premises, and the continuing partners are not yet in a position to buy these from him. By remaining a Schedule D partner, the outgoing partner preserves the possibility for retirement relief if he should sell the premises in a few years' time when he actually retires from the partnership (see chapter 15).

Change in status to salaried partner

If personalities permit, there could be some advantage for the outgoing partner to revert to a salaried partner status and be taxed under Schedule E. The timing of such a change may warrant some consideration, eg a partner expecting to retire in 1997/98 or 1998/99 may find it attractive to cease to be a Schedule D partner before the new regime takes effect (he will not then have to worry about the CY basis and the operation of transitional relief).

There can be other benefits from a switch from Schedule D status to Schedule E. The continuing partners could undertake to fund an approved pension scheme which in turn may enable a substantial tax-free lump sum to be provided in cases where the outgoing partner had previously been an employee (or a salaried partner). Benefits under an approved scheme must be related to periods of service as an employee but there is no statutory requirement that the periods be continuous as opposed to two periods separated by a period as a Schedule D partner.

The timing of any contributions into an approved scheme may need to be carefully considered. It will be less beneficial to the continuing partners if substantial contributions were to be made during the **transitional basis period** which will determine the firm's assessment for 1996/97, see p 39.

Consultancy arrangement

It could be that the individual will agree to retire from the firm only if he receives a 'retainer' under which the firm is committed to consult him (and pay him) for a minimum number of days' work for a specified period.

Unless the retainer is substantial, it is unusual for the Revenue to seek to classify an ex-partner consultant as an employee, notwithstanding that he may not undertake work for many other clients (if any). However, this possibility should be borne in mind and the consultancy agreement should be carefully drafted so as to avoid any suggestion of a 'master/servant' relationship. If there is any doubt, the partnership will need to withhold PAYE from the consultancy fees.

Whilst it may better suit the individual to be taxed as a consultant under Schedule D Case II, particularly if there are expenses that he can claim against his consultancy income such as the cost of maintaining an office in his home, payment to his wife for secretarial services and business use of a car, the firm must protect its position. In particular, where the consultancy fee exceeds the VAT threshold, the firm must obtain a valid VAT invoice.

To some extent, it may be better for the firm if the former partner receives an annuity as greater relief may be obtained in 1996/97.

EXAMPLE

Richard retires from the firm on 1 May 1995 and has a consultancy fee of £20,000 per annum.

Under the transitional basis period rules, the firm may effectively receive relief only on 50 per cent of the consultancy fees paid during the firm's year ended 30 April 1996 (see pp 38–40).

If Richard had received an annuity of £20,000, the partners would receive relief on the whole of the annuity payments made in the tax years 1995/96 and 1996/97.

Annuity arrangements

An annuity may effectively be paid out of pre-tax income since the payer will normally be entitled to relief at his marginal rate of tax. An annuity of £10,000 will be satisfied by the partners paying £7,500 (ie £10,000 less basic rate tax) and they will then be able to claim the full amount as a deduction in arriving at their total income for higher rate tax purposes.

As already mentioned, payment as an annuity may be more tax efficient than consultancy payments during the transitional basis period.

The main drawback with annuity payments is that the continuing partners cannot raise qualifying loans in order to meet these obligations.

So far as the outgoing partner is concerned, he may prefer a capital sum, especially where **retirement relief** or **roll-over relief** may be relevant. On the other hand, the annuity should not attract a capital gains tax liability provided it is within the limits laid down in the Revenue's *Statement of Practice* SP1/89 — see Chapter 7, Appendix 2.

Payment of a capital sum

A capital sum may be paid direct to an outgoing partner or an adverse balance on his capital account may be written off — this is in effect a capital payment by means of a transfer from the continuing partners' capital accounts.

Where one or more partners raise personal loans in order to buy out a colleague, interest will normally qualify for relief under ICTA 1988, s 362. If, exceptionally, the interest on such loans exceeds their partnership profits, the excess may be carried forward as if it were a Schedule D Case II loss.

Perhaps the most important aspect to consider is that if the buy-out does not succeed, and the borrower cases to carry on the practice, the loan will cease to qualify for tax purposes. This has been a real problem for the proprietors of firms which have subsequently got into financial difficulties.

Capital gains tax implications

A partner who is being bought out may have a potential capital gains tax unless he can make use of roll-over relief or his gain is covered by retirement relief (see Chapters 7 and 15).

In some situations, an out-going partner may retain an interest in the office premises from which the practice is carried on after he has retired from the partnership. This must be a commercial decision, but only limited roll-over relief will be available on a subsequent sale, and retirement relief may be forfeited altogether.

Continuation or cessation?

The fact that a partner is bought out may give rise to a deemed cessation if this takes place before 6 April 1997 — unless a **continuation election** is made or the firm is already on the CY basis. The implications of this need to be thought through very carefully — for more detail, see Chapter 2.

Splitting the practice

In some situations, the outgoing partner effectively takes over one particular office and continues to practice on his own account. This is a 'de-merger' situation which we deal with in Chapter 13.

Chapter 13

Mergers and de-mergers

In this chapter, we look at some of the potential problem areas where two firms of solicitors merge their practice.

•   Continuation or cessation of 'old firms'?
•   Position where only one firm is on the cash basis.
•   Qualifying loans.
•   Adjustments between current accounts.
•   Value Added Tax.
•   De-mergers.

Continuation or cessation of 'old firms'?

The position will change after 5 April 1997, but at present the treatment will normally follow the Revenue's *Statement of Practice* SP9/86 — see Appendix 1 to this chapter.

Basically, it is a matter of fact where two businesses merge as to whether the new firm carries on the business previously carried on by each firm. However, unless there is a great disparity in the size of the two firms, it will normally be possible to satisfy the Revenue that the merged firm is carrying on the businesses of the two predecessor firms. This will mean that the partners have the following options open to them:

(1) They can make **continuation elections** in respect of both firms.
(2) They can make a continuation election in respect of one firm but not the other (but it should be borne in mind that the Revenue will often resist this).
(3) They can have the merger treated as a cessation of both

of the predecessor firms and the merged firm will be treated as carrying on a new business.

We look at each situation in turn.

Continuation elections made by both firms

Where a continuation election is made by both firms, there will be no cessation and deemed commencement of a new practice. If the merger takes place in 1994/95, the assessment on the merged firm for 1995/96 will normally be based on the combined profits of the two predecessor firms for their years which end in 1994/95.

For 1996/97, the assessment will be based on 12 months' proportion of the profits for the firm's accounts which end in 1996/97 **plus** the profits earned by each firm during the period from the end of the basis period for 1995/96 up to the date of the merger.

The most straightforward situation is where both firms have the same accounting date. Thus, if two firms with a 31 March year end merge on 1 April 1995, the merged firm's tax assessment for 1995/96 will be the combined profits of both firms for the year ended 31 March 1995.

The position is more complicated where the firms have had different accounting dates, as the rules described in Chapter 3 must also be taken into account.

EXAMPLE

Foreman and partners have always made up their accounts to 31 December. Ross & Co have a 31 March accounting date. The two firms merge on 1 January 1995.

The profits for each firm are as follows:

	Foreman and Partners	Ross & Co
Year ended 31 March 1993		60,000
Year ended 31 December 1993	100,000	
Year ended 31 March 1994		80,000
Period 1 April–31 December 1994		32,000
Year ended 31 December 1994	120,000	

Merged Firm	£
Year ended 31 December 1995	220,000
Year ended 31 December 1996	300,000
Year ended 31 December 1997	360,000

The assessments will be as follows:

	Foreman & Partners	Ross & Co
1994/95	£	£
Profits for 6 April 1994 to 31 December 1994		
$9/12 \times £100,000$	75,000	
$9/12 \times £75,636$ (see example on pp 30–31)		56,727

Assessment on merged firm

1994/95
1 January 1995 to 5 April 1995

Foreman & Partnership ($3/12 \times £100,000$)	25,000
Ross & Co ($3/12 \times £75,636$) (Change of accounting date)	18,909
	43,909

1995/96

Foreman & Partners	120,000
Ross & Co (Change of accounting date)	52,000
	172,000

1996/97

Merged firm:

12 months to 31 December 1995	220,000
12 months to 31 December 1996	300,000
Profits of transitional year basis period	520,000
Assurance 1996/97 £520,000 $\times$ $12/24$ =	260,000

Continuation election made in respect of only one firm

The main implication of the partners in one of the predecessor firms accepting a cessation is that the Inland Revenue may adjust the assessments for the year of the merger and the two preceding years (see Chapter 2 re **closing years' rules**). However, they will then share in the assessment on the merged firm for the year in which the merger takes place and subsequent years until 1997/98.

EXAMPLE

James & Co merges their practice with Adrian and Partners on 1 December 1994. James & Co does not make a continuation election in respect of old firm, but a continuation election is made in respect of Adrian and Partners and the new firm. However, James & Co's share of the merged partnership is assessed under the commencement of business rules for a business starting after 5 April 1994.

The figures are as follows:

	James & Co £	Adrian and Partners £	Merged Firm £
Year ended 30 November 1991	70,000	110,000	
Year ended 30 November 1992	78,000	120,000	
Year ended 30 November 1993	156,000	144,000	
Year ended 30 November 1994	180,000	196,000	
Year ended 30 November 1995	195,000	165,000	360,000
Year ended 30 November 1996	200,000	208,000	408,000
Year ended 30 November 1997			600,000

The assessments will be as follows:

James & Co

The Inland Revenue will adjust the assessments for the two years prior to the year of the merger.

	PY	Actual
1992/93		
30 November 1991	70,000	
(£78,000 × $^8/_{12}$) + (£156,000 × $^4/_{12}$)		104,000
1993/94		
30 November 1992	78,000	
(£156,000 × $^8/_{12}$) + (£180,000 × $^4/_{12}$)		164,000
	148,000	268,000

Consequently, the Revenue will adjust the assessments for 1992/93 and 1993/94 to an actual basis.

Effect of merger

Because there is no continuation election, the new rules apply to the profits attributable to James & Co's share of the practice with effect from the merger date. Adrian & Partners remain assessable under the existing rules (PY basis for 1995/96, transitional year 1996/97, then CY basis) by virtue of its continuation election. The assessments therefore become:

1994/95 (6 April 1994 to 30 November 1994)

	James & Co £	Adrian & Partners £
£180,000 × 8/12	120,000	
£144,000 × 8/12		96,000

	Merged Firm £
1 December 1994 to 5 April 1995	
James & Co (£195,000 × 4/12)	65,000
Adrian & Partners (£144,000 × 4/12)	48,000
	113,000
1995/96	
James & Co — year ended 30 November 1995	195,000
Adrian & Partners — year ended 30 November 1994	196,000
	391,000
1996/97	
James & Co — year ended 30 November 1996	200,000
Adrian & Partners — ½ × (2 years ended 30 November 1996)	186,500
	386,500
1997/98	
Year ended 30 November 1997	600,000

No continuation election made at all

In many ways, this is the simplest situation. Each predecessor firm is deemed to have ceased to practise at the time of the merger. The **closing year rules** may enable the Revenue to amend the assessments for the penultimate and ante-penultimate years (see Chapter 2 re closing years' rules). As regards the merged firm, each partner will be separately assessed on the basis that the new rules will apply in relation to the merged firm as if it were a completely new practice.

Practical problems may arise where both of the predecessor firms were on the cash basis. The merged firm must produce accounts on the earnings basis and wait for three years before moving back on to the cash basis.

Another potential problem is where expenses may arise in future in relation to one of the predecessor firms, eg liability to pay rent under a lease which was assigned and where the assignee has failed to pay the rent.

Position where only one firm is on the cash basis

Practical problems may also arise where one of the firms is on the cash basis. There is an income tax charge on post cessation receipts arising from the unpaid bills and work-in-progress of a cash basis firm which ceases its business or which is deemed to have done so by virtue of the merger, or changes from the cash to the earnings basis. A merger of two firms will automatically result in one of these events occurring unless the new firm adopts the cash basis and continuation elections are made in respect of both businesses.

The great disadvantage of switching from the earnings basis to the cash basis is that some income is charged twice. The firm which was formerly on the earnings basis will have paid tax on profits which took account of the firm's unpaid bills and work-in-progress but these sums will attract tax all over again when the cash is eventually received.

EXAMPLE

Coke & Co and Mansfield and partners merge their practices on 1 January 1995. Coke & Co formerly produced accounts including debtors and work-in-progress and the amount at 31 December 1995 was

£300,000. Mansfield and partners are on the cash basis. If the new firm adopts the cash basis the £300,000 will be taxed again as a receipt for 1995 or a later period (if the fees are received after 31 December 1995). In one sense, this will not be an immediate problem since the Inland Revenue will only tax one full year's profits at a time as the closing debtors and work-in-progress at each year end will not be charged.

However, when the firm ceases business in (say) January 1999 the closing work-in-progress will be charged as a post cessation receipt. By that time the original partners may have long since retired!

The alternative is for the new firm to adopt the earnings basis, but this will mean that the former partners in Mansfield and partners will pay tax on a full year's profits **plus** amounts which were invoiced by Mansfield and partners, but only received after the merger has gone through. This may be less unattractive if it occurs during the transitional year as substantially increased profits may then be balanced by increased transitional relief.

Qualifying loans

Partners who have raised loans in connection with a predecessor firm and which qualify under ICTA 1988, s 362 may continue to obtain relief for interest.

The part of Extra Statutory Concession A43 which is relevant to partnerships (as opposed to investors in companies) reads as follows:

Interest relief: investments in partnerships

1. Under sections 360–363 of the Income and Corporation Taxes Act 1988, income tax relief is available for interest paid by an individual on a loan taken out to invest in, or on-lend to, a partnership, a co-operative, a close company, or an employee-controlled company. The relief is subject to various conditions, and ceases to be available when those conditions are no longer met.

2. Relief is also reduced or withdrawn (following s 363) if the borrower recovers any capital from the business without using it to repay the loan — for example by selling or exchanging the

interest or shares in that business. Strictly, therefore, relief ceases to be due where:

...(c)   there is a partnership reconstruction involving a merger or demerger.

3.   Under the terms of this concession, **relief for interest on a loan to an individual will not be discontinued in the circumstances described above** where, in relation to that individual, the conditions for relief would have met if the loan had been a new loan taken out by that person to invest in the new business entity. The rules restricting or withdrawing relief where the borrower recovers any capital from the business continue to apply in the normal way'.

Adjustments between current accounts

The past is a foreign country; they do things differently there! One of the practical problems with mergers is that each firm may have long established practices which have operated equitably, but are considered inappropriate in the merged firm. For example, there may have been a policy that all partners should be insured for a set amount, with the costs spread amongst the partners. This would have been achieved by treating the cost as a disallowable expense like entertaining, but in the merged practice equity may necessitate that the relevant amount should be debited to each partner's account.

Other situations where adjustments may be required between partners' current accounts are:

●   Post merger liabilities arising from pre-merger activities to be borne by the (former) partners of the appropriate firm;
●   Adjustments to establish a common approach in valuing work in progress;
●   Inter-firm payments to reflect inequality in the value of assets contributed by each practice;
●   Releases of specific pre-merger provisions no longer required.

Some of these items may be taxable or tax deductible as appropriate whilst others may not. It is, therefore, important always to consider the nature and effects of profits and loss account items taken direct to partners' current accounts and the impact of any inter-partner adjustments to ensure the correct tax effect is achieved.

EXAMPLE

The merger agreement between Elias Smith & Co and

Jones & Co provided that a £25,000 provision against a specific debt would belong to the Elias Smith partners in the event it was not needed. After two years, Elias Smith Jones & Co recover the debt in full and the provision is credited direct to the current accounts of the former Elias Smith partners.

Since this credit by-passed the profit and loss account, an adjustment needs to be made in the tax computations to increase taxable profits by £25,000, allocating this between the Elias Smith partners.

If, instead, the payment had gone through profit and loss account it would have been necessary to effect an inter-partner adjustment to transfer from the Jones & Co partners to the Elias Smith partners the element of profit shares attributable to the £25,000 released provision.

Value Added Tax

A partnership is treated as a separate legal entity under the VAT legislation. Where two businesses merge, the partners can either:

- De-register one practice and amend the registration of the other to include the in-coming partners; or
- De-register both practices and register the merged practice from the date of the merger.

In practice, the most appropriate action may depend upon how the merger is to be treated for Inland Revenue purposes.

Normally, the transfer of going concern provisions will be met and there will be no VAT charged on the transfer of assets.

De-mergers

The normal treatment where partners buy out an office is for them to be treated as starting a new practice. The partners in the main firm can avoid a cessation by making a continuation election. However, it may be possible to satisfy the Revenue that a de-merger consists of separating two businesses which were different businesses all along. Thus, if a firm of solicitors consists of five offices in different towns, it could be argued that one particular office was a distinct practice whose departure from the rest of the partnership need not involve a commencement of a new business. This would enable both the continuing partners in the main firm and the partner(s) who have taken on the office which has de-merged to make continuation elections — or indeed for the main firm to have a cessation and for the de-merger parties to make a continuation election.

Capital Gains Tax

The de-merger parties will normally have a disposal of their interest in the assets of the main firm and an acquisition of an enlarged interest in the assets of the de-merged firm. Depending upon the relative values, any capital gains may well be covered by roll-over relief. See on this paragraphs 2–4 of the Revenue's *Statement of Practice* of 17 March 1975 — Appendix 2 to Chapter 7.

Value Added Tax

As partners are jointly and severally liable for VAT, it is important to notify Customs of the outgoing partners immediately the de-merger takes effect. Joint and several liability continues up to the date that the change is notified.

Appendix 1 — Inland Revenue Statement of Practice SP 9/86: partnerships mergers and demergers

1. This statement explains the basis on which the Revenue apply the provisions of s 113 ICTA 1988 (change in ownership of trade, profession or vocation) to mergers and demergers of partnership businesses. In the following paragraphs, the word 'business' means trades, professions or vocations carried on in partnership.

Mergers

2. When two businesses which are carried on in partnership and which are different in nature merge, it may be that the result of the merger is a new business, different in nature from either of the previous businesses. Whether this is so is a question of fact to be determined according to the circumstances of each case. Where it is the case, the old businesses will have been permanently discontinued, and a new business commenced; s 113 ICTA 1988 will therefore not apply and the normal commencement and cessation provisions will apply to each business respectively.

3. However, where two partnership businesses in different ownership carrying on the same sort of activities are merged and then carried on by the joint owners in partnership, the total activities of both businesses may continue, even though in a merged form, ie the new partnership may succeed to the businesses of the old partnerships. In that event the partners have the following options:

   (*a*) s 113 ICTA 1988 applies to both businesses so that the cessation and commencement provisions are deemed to apply to both;

   (*b*) an election under s 113 ICTA 1988 is made in respect of one business, and the cessation and commencement provisions are deemed to apply to the other;

   (*c*) elections are made in respect of both businesses.

4. Where (*b*) applies, it will be necessary to apportion the profits of the combined business to apply the commencement provisions to the business in respect of which no election

is made. It will of course be a question of fact whether succession has occurred and in this connection disparity in size between the old partnerships will not of itself be a significant matter.

Demergers

5. When a business carried on in partnership is divided up, and several separate partnerships are formed, it will again be a question of fact, to be determined according to the circumstances of each case, whether any of the separate partnerships carries on the same business as was carried on previously by the original partnership. It might be that one of the businesses carried on after the division was so large in relation to the rest as to be recognisably 'the business' as previously carried on; but that will frequently not be the case, and if it is not the case an election under s 113 ICTA 1988 will not be possible.

6. The Revenue would want to look carefully at any case where it was claimed that a demerger of a partnership had occurred but it appeared that the demerger was more apparent than real, and that the demerger seemed to have taken place for fiscal reasons. The Revenue might wish to argue that in such a case the same trade was being carried on after the demerger as before, that a s 113 ICTA 1988 election could be made, and that s 61 ICTA 1988 therefore applied.

Part IV

Planning for retirement

In this section, we look at the legislation on relief for contributions into personal pension schemes and retirement annuity policies. We also look at the tax consequences of retirement and possible ways of maximising capital gains tax retirement relief.

14 Pension provision.

15 Retirement from the firm.

Chapter 14

Pension provision

As a sole practitioner or a partner in a professional firm, you will not be able to participate under an approved pension scheme for employees. It follows that if you wish to fund a pension, you will need to take out a personal pension policy or make contributions to a retirement annuity policy.

In this chapter, we look at the rules governing personal pension policies and retirement annuity contributions. We also look at the possibilities for 'self-invested' pension plans.

- Personal pension plans
- Retirement annuity policies
- Transfers out of staff pension schemes
- Self-investment

Personal pension plans

Personal pension plans were introduced in July 1988. The legislation is now contained in ICTA 1988, ss 630–655. The rules are summarised below:

Scheme administrator

A personal pension plan must have a scheme administrator. This can be one of the following:

- An insurance company.
- A unit trust group.
- A friendly society.
- A building society or bank.

Benefits

The benefits can be taken at any time between ages 50 and 75. Up to 25 per cent of the value of the fund may be taken as a lump sum which is free of tax. The other 75 per cent (or more) of the fund must be used to purchase an annuity.

Maximum contributions

Contributions may be made at the following rate for the current year:

Individual's age at the beginning of the year of assessment	Maximum Contributions
Under 36	17.5%
36–45	20%
46–50	25%
51–55	30%
56–60	35%
61 or more	40%

The above limits came into effect from 1989/90. For 1988/89 the limits were:

Individual's age at the beginning of the year of assessment	Maximum Contributions
Up to 50	17.5%
51–55	20%
56–60	22.5%
61 or more	27.5%

The above percentages refer to the individual's 'relevant earnings' for a tax year. Relevant earnings include earnings from a non-pensionable employment as well as earnings from self-employment so if you have recently been appointed a partner, and you were not previously in a staff pension scheme, your relevant earnings include your remuneration as an employee.

EXAMPLE

James is appointed as a partner in Mansfield & Partners on 1 January 1995. His share of the firm's profits for 1994/95 is £20,000.

Previously, he was a manager in Coke & Co and had a pensionable salary of £50,000. He left this position in July 1994 and took up a new position as a manager with Mansfield & Partners which was not pensionable.

James's relevant earnings for 1994/95 are his earnings as a manager with Mansfield & Partners during the period July–December 1994. The salary from Coke & Co would also have been relevant earnings but for the fact that James was a member of their pension scheme.

An employment is not regarded as pensionable if the only benefits provided under the pension scheme consist of a lump sum payable on death in service. Furthermore, even if James had been eligible to join the Mansfield & Partners pension scheme, his earnings would still be relevant earnings if he had chosen not to join.

Earnings cap

There is a limit or cap to the amount of an individual's relevant earnings. The limit is increased year by year and is at present £76,800.
   The limits for earlier years are as follows:

	£
1989/90	60,000
1990/91	64,800
1991/92	71,400
1992/93 and 1993/94	75,000

Carry forward from earlier years

If you have not taken full advantage of your ability to make personal
pension contributions in earlier years, the excess may be carried
forward. Once you have made the maximum contributions for the
current year, you can make further contributions to utilise unused
relief brought forward from the previous six years.

EXAMPLE

Jack is aged 34. He has paid no personal pension
contributions whatsoever except for a lump sum payment
of £5,000 in 1991/92. His relevant earnings are:

	£
1987/88	100,000
1988/89	30,000
1989/90	20,000
1990/91	40,000
1991/92	44,000
1992/93	50,000
1993/94	35,000
1994/95	45,000

Jack can pick up utilised relief for earlier years only if he makes
the maximum contribution of the current year (1994/95). The
maximum he could pay is £41,200 (£7,875 based on 1994/95 relevant
earnings and £33,325 as unutilised relief brought forward, computed
as follows:

	£	
1987/88	Nil	(out of date)
1988/89	5250	(17.5% of £30,000)
1989/90	3500	(17.5% of £20,000)
1990/91	7000	(17.5% of £40,000)
1991/92	2700	(17.5% of £44,000 less contribution paid of £5,000)
1992/93	8750	(17.5% of £50,000)
1993/94	6125	(17.5% of £35,000)
	£33,325	

If Jack paid £20,000 instead of £33,325, he would use his 1994/95 relief, the unused relief for 1988/89–1989/90 and £3,345 of his unused relief for 1990/91.

Relating back

It is possible to make a pension contribution and 'relate it back' to the preceding year. The election to carry-back must be lodged with the Inland Revenue by 5 July following the end of the tax year in which the contribution is paid.

In the above example, Jack could elect for his contribution to be related back to 1993/94. It would then use the 1993/94 relief of 17.5% of £35,000 and (if the contribution exceeds £6,125) he can utilise unused relief for 1987/88 (which would be in date if used in 1993/94) and for the years 1988/89–1992/93.

If you had no relevant earnings in the preceding tax year, you may relate back contributions to the year before that. Thus, if Jack retired in 1994/95, he may relate back to 1994/95 contributions paid in 1996/97.

There is a planning point here. Under the **current year basis**, a partner's assessable income for the year in which he retires from a firm may be substantially reduced by **overlap relief** or **transitional relief**. In order to derive the maximum benefit from pension contributions, it may well be appropriate to relate back contributions to the year preceding the year of retirement.

Life assurance

Up to five per cent of an individual's relevant earnings may be paid into a personal pension policy which provides life assurance. However, amounts paid over in this connection use up part of the individual's annual limit, so that if the individual can pay 17.5 per cent in a year, a payment of five per cent to procure life assurance would mean that he can pay only 12.5 per cent into a normal personal pension scheme.

Retirement annuity policies

These policies are similar to personal pension plans. In effect, they were a predecessor to personal pension plans and no new policy taken out after 1 July 1988 can be a retirement annuity policy. However, most retirement annuity policies issued before that date allow additional premiums to be paid and so it will be some years before individuals no longer make contributions under retirement annuity policies.

The following limits apply to contributions made under retirement annuity policies:

Individual's age at the beginning of the year of assessment	Maximum Contributions
up to 50	17.5%
51–55	20%
56–60	22.5%
61 or more	27.5%

There is no earnings cap for retirement annuity policies.

EXAMPLE

Fiona is aged 52 and has relevant earnings of £210,000. She can pay £42,000 into a retirement annuity policy but only £23,040 into a personal pension plan (30 per cent of £76,800).

Potential problem area

Care is required where an individual pays a mixture of personal pension premiums and retirement annuity contributions. Doing this can result in the earnings cap applying in situations where an individual could pay larger amounts if he made contributions only under a retirement annuity policy. This is an area where you should take advice from a specialist.

Transfers out of staff pension schemes

It is possible to convert your entitlement under a staff pension scheme into a lump sum payment into a personal pension scheme.

The decision as to whether to take a transfer value will depend upon a number of factors, ie your age, whether the staff pension scheme is a final salary scheme, and the level of benefits provided. There is no general rule, but if you are relatively young (ie younger than 40) and the staff scheme is a money purchase scheme, it may be more appropriate for you to take a transfer value into your personal pension scheme. Where a transfer has been taken in this way, the benefits may be taken under the Personal Pension Scheme rules — ie at any time after the individual attains age 50.

Self-investment

Until recently self-investment could be achieved only via a special unit-linked insurance fund or a friendly society arrangement. The way that each of these schemes worked and some of the limiting factors are set out below as this type of scheme may still operate within your firm. In 1989, the Revenue published regulations concerning self-invested personal pension plans and these regulations govern any new arrangement.

'Closed' or 'private' unit-linked funds

Some insurance companies operated 'closed' unit-linked retirement annuity funds which were open only to partners in a particular firm and who contributed premiums to the insurance company. The insurance company is the legal owner of any such investments but the partners have a degree of control over the investment policy. The fund can, however, only acquire investments approved by the Pension Schemes Office. These are normally quoted investments, and commercial property (including, in certain circumstances, premises used by the firm).

The following ground rules apply to such schemes.

1) Possible investments are restricted by the Insurance Companies Act 1974 and the Insurance Companies (Linked Properties and Indices) Regulations 1975. As mentioned above, commercial property is commonly purchased and rented back to the partnership for their use, but investment in residential property is strictly forbidden.
2) If a partnership occupies property owned by the pension fund, this must be an arm's length transaction and a commercial rent must be paid to the pension fund.
3) As the pension fund is completely exempt from tax, there will be no capital gains tax liability on the sale of the property. However, whilst this benefit is attractive, it should not be overestimated. There can often be circumstances where the

disposal by a retiring partner of his interest in the property would be exempt from capital gains tax anyway, eg because of retirement relief (see p 188).

4)   Problems may arise where one of the partners leaves the partnership before retirement as the benefits cannot be taken at this time. It will generally be inappropriate for the ex-partner to have an investment in the fund managed by the remaining partners. Where an insurance company is involved, a switch to units in one of its other unit-linked funds may be possible, provided that the cash flow situation within the partnership scheme will permit this.

5)   A pension mortgage or 'loan back' will not generally be available to partners and this may be a serious drawback for new partners who wish to use this source of finance to purchase their share of the partnership.

Friendly society arrangements

As an alternative to the self-managed schemes for self-employed persons, some firms used friendly societies. This avoided the involvement of an insurance company and provided the same tax benefits.

In order to be able to take advantage of this, the partners had to fulfil the following conditions:

1)   The firm had to have at least seven partners who were required to establish the arrangement and obtain approval for the Friendly Society from the Chief Registrar of Friendly Societies.

2)   The actual personal pension policy document required approval by the Inland Revenue.

3)   The Registrar requires audited annual returns for the scheme.

The Trustee Investments Act 1961 requires at least 50 per cent of the fund to be invested in 'narrow range' investments and the managers need to ensure that their investments comply with these provisions.

Personal pension plans

The Pension Schemes Office published its views on self-invested and self-managed personal pension plans in Memorandum No 101, issued in October 1989. This stated that:

> Decisions on the extent of choice which schemes members can have are matters for each scheme to decide. There will be no Revenue requirements on this point. Some schemes may choose to limit individual involvement to selecting the parameters of the investment portfolio, leaving the selection of particular investments to a fund manager. On the other hand, others may give the members a direct say as to the specific investment to be held and when they should be bought or sold.
>
> The Pension Schemes Office will now consider for approval those schemes whose rules allow members to choose the underlying investments. The choice will, however, not be unlimited, and the investments will be restricted to: quoted securities; unlisted securities; market stocks and shares; securities quoted on a recognised overseas stock exchange; unit trusts and investment trusts; deposit accounts; and commercial property.

Furthermore, certain investments are specifically prohibited:

- Loans must not be made to members or any persons connected with a member. Furthermore, 'no loan from any source made to an individual who is a member of the scheme should in any way affect the return on the investments representing that member's interest in the scheme'.
- Schemes must not acquire investments from members or sell assets to them.
- Investments may not be made in residential property.

Commercial property may be leased to a partnership or business connected with the members only if the terms of the lease are determined by a professional valuation. Unfortunately, the rules on Self Invested Personal Pension Plans do not allow the scheme to purchase office premises already owned by the firm, but it may well be that the scheme can acquire a lease where the firm moves into new premises or, indeed, when an opportunity comes up to acquire premises which the firm presently rents.

Chapter 15

Retirement from the firm

In this chapter, we look at the capital gains tax implications of a sale of your practice or interest in a partnership. We also cover the income tax treatment of post cessation receipts and annuities paid by former partners.

SOLE PRACTITIONERS

- Terminal loss relief.
- Post-cessation receipts (and expenses).
- Potential problem areas.
- CGT Retirement relief for sole practitioners.
- Planning ahead for retirement after 5 April 1997.

PARTNERS

- Terminal loss relief.
- CGT Retirement relief for partners.
- Tax treatment of annuities paid to former partners.
- Advance planning for retirement after 5 April 1997.

SOLE PRACTITIONERS

Terminal loss relief

Loss relief is extended in cases where the loss arises during the final 12 months of business. In such a situation, the loss may be carried back and set against profits of the business for the previous three years. The loss must be set against the profits of the most recent year first.

EXAMPLE

Sidney retires from practice on 5 April 1995. He has a loss of £13,000 for the final 12 months. If he claims terminal loss relief, the loss must be set first against Sidney's Schedule D Case II assessment for 1993/94 and only if there is any balance which is unused may the loss be carried back to 1992/93 or 1991/92.

Post-cessation receipts (and expenses)

Where a person has been assessed on the **cash basis** special rules apply if the trade or profession is discontinued. Subsequent receipts are normally taxed under Schedule D Case VI as income for the year in which they come in, although an election may be made for the post-cessation receipts to be treated as arising in the year of discontinuance.

Expenses may be deducted in so far as they were incurred wholly and exclusively for business purposes and are not otherwise allowable. For example, a solicitor who had post-cessation receipts would be able to deduct premiums paid on a professional indemnity policy where the cover related to the period after the solicitor had ceased to carry on his profession.

It is possible to make further contributions to personal pension schemes (or retirement annuity policies) based on post cessation receipts which are taxed under Schedule D Case VI.

Potential problem areas

We have touched on one potential pitfall already. Where a former sole practitioner is required to make a payment after he has ceased to practice, there may be no tax relief. Thus, to take one example, where a sole practitioner is required to pay rent for the remainder of a lease, he will not be entitled to a deduction unless his accounts were prepared on the cash basis. Even then, relief is limited to a deduction against any post-cessation receipts (see above).

Another area where problems can arise is if a sole practitioner assigns his lease and the assignee ceases to meet his obligations. The landlord will then normally be able to call upon the original leaseholder to pay the outstanding rent and service charges and there will be no relief where the practitioner has ceased to practice before such a contingent liability becomes payable.

CGT retirement relief for sole practitioners

This is an important relief which may be available under TCGA 1992, s 163 on the sale of a practice (or other business). The relief is normally available only if the individual is aged at least 55 or is having to retire early because of ill health.

The maximum relief is £250,000 plus a further amount of 50 per cent of gains in excess of £250,000 (up to an overall ceiling of £1m). The £250,000 and £1m limits came into force on 30 November 1993, prior to that the limits were £150,000 and £600,000.

Retirement through ill health

The legislation provides that retirement relief should be available to an individual who is being required to dispose of his business before he attains age 55 because ill health makes it impossible for him to carry on.

In practice, the Revenue requires claimants to provide a medical certificate, signed by a qualified medical practitioner (whether or not the claimant's own general practitioner). The Board will themselves take advice from the Regional Medical Service of the Department of Health, and in some cases a further medical examination by the Regional Medical Officer will be required.

The Revenue have made it clear that retirement relief will not be given to someone aged below 55 where he has ceased work because of the ill health of someone else, eg his spouse.

Ten year period

The maximum relief is based on all of the requirements being met for a period of ten years. The relief is tapered using the 'appropriate percentage' which starts off at ten per cent for one year and rises to 100 per cent for the full ten years.

EXAMPLE

Philip who is 57 years old and fulfils all of the conditions, disposes of his practice. He has owned this for seven years and so he is entitled to exemption on a capital gain of up to $7/_{10} \times £250,000$, ie £175,000. Half of any gains between £175,000 and £700,000 will also be exempt.

If Philip had owned the practice for ten years, the full £250,000 and £1m limits would have applied.

However, it is possible to aggregate periods spent running different businesses. This means that relief may be increased where the individual has been in business as a sole practitioner or partner or a full-time director or employee of a personal trading company. Thus, if Philip had been a director of a personal trading company (ie a company where he held at least five per cent of the voting shares), for three years and then he acquired the practice, he might be entitled to the full retirement relief rather than only $\frac{7}{10}$ths.

Planning ahead for retirement after 5 April 1997

It will generally be beneficial for the profits of the transitional period to be as large as possible — provided the individual will retire within the reasonably near future or there is some other way of utilising transitional relief.

The computation of transitional relief may be affected by the date on which an individual retires in 1997/98. The basic rule is that where an individual has two accounting periods ending in 1997/98, they are treated as a single period. This can produce major differences if profits increase during 1997/98.

EXAMPLE

Louise makes up accounts to 30 April. Her profits for the year ended 30 April 1997 amount to £120,000. Normally, her transitional relief will be $\frac{340}{365}$ × £120,000 ie £111,781.

However, if Louise ceases practice on 31 March 1998, and her profits for the 11 months amount to £340,000, the transitional relief becomes:

$$\frac{340}{365 + 335 \text{ days}} \times £460,000 \text{ ie } £223,428$$

On the other hand, a sole practitioner will need to take care to ensure that his retirement in 1997/98 or 1998/99 does not allow the Revenue the option to adjust the assessments for 1995/96 and 1996/97. One possible strategy is to look for someone who will be prepared to join in a partnership for a few months, and who will then continue the practice at least until 6 April 1999.

PARTNERS

Terminal loss relief

A retiring partner may be entitled to terminal loss relief even though the firm continues. Moreover, the loss can be carried back and set against profits of the firm for periods prior to a cessation having taken place because of a change in partners.

CGT retirement relief for partners

Relief may be available to a partner who retires after attaining age 55 or who retires early because of ill-health (the same rules apply as for sole practitioners, see above). However, retirement relief may be available even though the partner does not in fact retire since a gain may attract retirement relief where it arises on a disposal which takes place on the introduction of a new partner or on some other change in profit sharing ratios combined with a revaluation of partnership assets.

As with sole practitioners, full relief is available only if the necessary conditions are satisfied for a minimum period of ten years ending with the date of the disposal. This ten year period may be made up of different periods provided they are not separated by more than two years.

EXAMPLE

Alan who was a sole practitioner from 1979 to 1982, then a partner in a firm which took over that practice from 1983 to 1989, and then a sole practitioner from 1990 to 1995 is treated as meeting the necessary conditions for the full ten year period even though his second period as a sole practitioner may have lasted only four years.

There are, however, potential pitfalls here in that if Alan had become a salaried partner from 1990 until 1993, and had then become a sole practitioner, the period from 1990 to 1993 would not qualify. Furthermore, because the periods from 1979–1989 and from 1994–1995 would have been separated by more than two years Alan could not combine them in order to claim a combined period of ten years. In this situation, the maximum retirement relief available would be $\frac{2}{10}$ of £250,000 ie $\frac{\text{1994–1995 (2 years)}}{\text{10 years}}$

In some cases, a partner may own an asset which is used by his firm, eg the office premises. Retirement relief is also available to cover a gain arising from the disposal of such an asset provided the following conditions are satisfied:

1) The disposal of the asset must take place as part of the withdrawal of the individual from participation in the business carried on by the partnership (once again this may include a reduction in his profit shares); and

2) The asset must have been used for the purposes of the partnership business immediately before the disposal (or the cessation of the business). A recent case has demonstrated that this test may be satisfied even where there is a short interval between the sale of the asset and the subsequent sale of the individual's interest in the firm.

Relief may be restricted where the partner has charged rent to the firm. The legislation provides that relief shall be restricted on a 'just and reasonable' basis.

EXAMPLE

Colin, Tony and Ian have been in partnership sharing profits equally. Ian owns the office premises and charges a rent of £10,000. He realises a gain of £120,000 on selling the premises when he retires from the firm.

If the £10,000 is a full commercial rent, then Ian will only be entitled to retirement relief on one third of his gain. The thinking here is that a partner cannot be treated as charging himself rent, so a proportion of the commercial rent charged to the firm is effectively ignored — the proportion reflecting that partner's profit sharing ratio.

On the other hand, if the full commercial rent is £25,000, a larger proportion of any capital gain will be eligible for retirement relief. In this case, the restriction would be as follows:

$$\frac{\text{rent charged}}{\text{commercial rent}} \times \frac{\text{proportion borne}}{\text{by other partners}} \times \text{capital gains}$$

$$\text{ie} \quad {}^{10}\!/_{25} \times {}^{2}\!/_{3} \times \text{£120,000} = \text{£32,000}$$

This means that out of his capital gain of £120,000, Ian may claim retirement relief on £88,000 and must pay tax in the normal way on £32,000.

One possible way in which a partner may increase his entitlement to retirement relief where he has charged rent in the past is by his converting the property into a partnership asset. Thus, in the above example, Ian could introduce the office premises into the firm as a partnership asset, but on the basis that the partnership deed were varied so that his entitlement to profits should reflect the rent that he will have forgone and on the basis that he will be entitled to (say) 99 per cent of any capital profits on a future disposal of the premises by the firm.

Tax treatment of annuities paid to former partners

The legislation provides that annuities shall be treated as earned income of the recipient provided they fall within certain limits. The conditions which need to be satisfied are as follows:

1) The payment must be made under the provisions of a partnership agreement, or an agreement replacing or supplementing the partnership agreement or an agreement with a person who purchased the whole or part of the partnership business; and

2) The payment must not exceed 50 per cent of the average of the former partner's share of profits for the best three of the last seven years in which he was required to devote substantially the whole of his time to the partnership.

For these purposes, profits are those before capital allowances. Any non-taxable profits or gains (eg repayment supplement) are included as if they were taxable. The actual profits can be adjusted in line with the Retail Price Index.

EXAMPLE

Andrew had Schedule D Case II profits of £60,000 for 1989/90, £70,000 for 1990/91, and £100,000 for 1991/92. There was also a non-taxable profit of £2,000 in 1991/92. After making adjustments for the Retail Price Index these figures become £75,000, £82,000 and £113,000 (£102,000 increased by RPI).

The average thereof is £90,000 and an annuity of up to £45,000 can therefore be treated as earned income. Any excess is treated as investment income.

It should be noted that, once payable, the annuity can itself increase in line with the Retail Price Index. There is no tax requirement that it should do so, but if it does the full annuity can be treated as earned income. It is less critical under the present tax regime that income be treated as earned income but this may change again in the future so it is still desirable from the point of view of the retired partner that his annuity should qualify as earned income.

Capital gains tax

The agreement to pay such an annuity is technically consideration for the disposal of goodwill, and therefore potentially subject to capital gains tax. However, the capitalised value of the annuity is not treated as consideration which is subject to capital gains tax provided:

1) The annuity does not exceed two thirds of the ex-partner's average share of profits for the best three of the last seven years in which he was required to devote substantially all his time to the business; and
2) He was a partner for at least ten years (or a partner in a firm which merged into the firm paying the annuity).

Where the annuitant was not a partner for ten years, the following limit may apply to the annuity:

Complete years of service as a partner	Fraction
1–5	1/60 for each year
6	8/60
7	16/60
8	24/60
9	32/60

194 *Partnership tax planning for solicitors*

Where a partner receives a capital sum and an annuity, the Inland Revenue practice is to take 1/9 of the lump sum and the annuity. If the aggregate does not exceed the above limits, no capital gains tax is charged on the capitalised value of the annuity (see Inland Revenue *Statement of Practice*, SP 1/79).

EXAMPLE

Clare retires after having completed nine years as a partner. She receives an annuity of £35,000 and a lump sum of £90,000. The average of the best three of her last seven years' profits is £56,000 (the *Statement of Practice* does not permit any indexation adjustment). $^{32}/_{60}$ of £56,000 amounts to £29,867.

Clare will be subject to capital gains tax on the actual consideration of £90,000 and notional consideration of the capitalised value of annuity in so far as it exceeds £19,867 (ie $^{32}/_{60}$ × £56,000 less £10,000 re lump sum).

If there had been no lump sum the notional consideration would be calculated as:

	£
Annuity	35,000
Less $^{32}/_{60}$ × £56,000	(29,867)
Capitalised value treated as consideration	5,133
Capitalised value thereof — say	£70,000

Any gain on the capitalised value of the annuity may be covered by **retirement relief** (see above), but this will not always be the case.

Advance planning for retirement after 5 April 1997

An individual who is approaching retirement should be taking all possible steps to ensure that his transitional relief is as much as possible. In some cases, this will need careful monitoring to see whether transitional relief will be increased by retirement on (say) 31 March 1998 rather than 30 April 1998 (see pp 43 and 189).

Ensure that cash will be available to repay any qualifying loans which will cease to qualify on your retiring as a partner (see p 142).

An older partner should also make advance preparations so that he can fully utilise unused personal pension relief for earlier years and be able to make substantial contributions in the tax year before retirement — or be able to relate back contributions made during the year of retirement from the firm (see p 181).

Finally, review the position on roll-over relief and retirement relief to ensure that gains are not going to arise on your leaving the firm or, if significant gains will occur, that they will be covered by retirement relief.

Index